Rosie Learns About

the

SOLAR SYSTEM

An Easy Introduction to Astronomy

by Diane Kirkpatrick

Table of Contents

Preface

An introduction to the solar system for elementary-aged children. More than just pictures, this book explains concepts and with clear writing and diagrams. Follow Dad, Rosie, Jane and Michael as they experience science first hand. *Rosie Learns about the Solar System* is a conversation between family members as they learn about their world, ask questions, and help each other love learning about science.

Moon Craters

"Time for a walk," Dad said.

The kids looked up from their TV show and groaned.

"Bundle up," he said. "It is finally a clear night."

The kids, Michael, Jane and Rosie, reluctantly followed him outside.

They huddled in their jackets, their breath visible in the chilly air.

The dog bounded ahead of them, happily chasing invisible cats.

"It's too dark," Rosie said. "I can't see where I'm going."

Dad pointed up at the sky.

"See the moon up there?" he asked. "It is lighting our way."

Rosie stared at the glowing circle.

The moon was just above the tops of the eastern mountains.

She watched it as they walked around the block.

When they got back home, Rosie stayed outside.

"Why does the moon have all those smudges on it?" she asked.

Dad smiled. "Those smudges are called craters. Some of the craters are big enough to be seen from earth without a telescope."

"What are craters like?" Rosie asked.

"They are big valleys on the moon. They are made when asteroids or meteors slam into the surface hard enough to leave marks."

Rosie looked confused.

"Come inside and I will show you some pictures."

Rosie nodded her head, and followed her Dad to the den.

He took a book off the shelf. It was a space atlas. The space atlas was full of pictures of planets and stars. He turned the pages until he found a large picture of the moon.

"There are more craters than I thought," Rosie said.

"Yes and they come in all shapes and sizes," Dad said.

"The big dark ones look like they could be oceans."

"The first scientists who looked at the moon thought so too. They called the biggest craters seas. But they are not filled with water."

"What is in them?" Rosie asked.

"Many years ago, many meteors hit the moon in the same place. These impact basins became very deep. Then, lava from ancient volcanoes flowed into the basins. That is why they look darker and flatter than the rest of the moon."

Rosie looked at the words on the diagram.

"I like the names, Sea of Serenity, Sea of Storms, Sea of Tranquility, Sea of Clouds, Sea of Showers. They sound so pretty," she said.

"Scientists named the craters that way because they believed the moon was a beautiful place."

Craters on the moon.

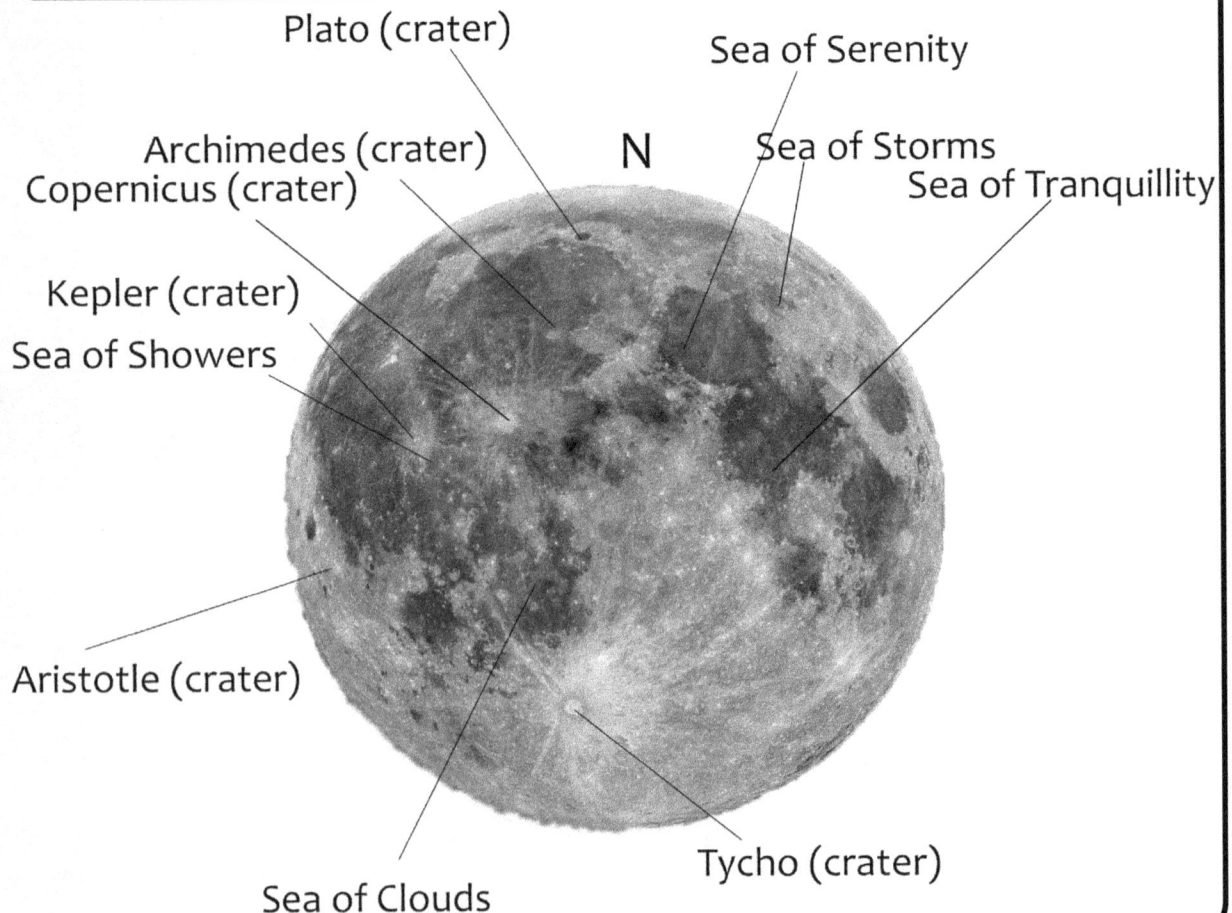

Plato (crater)

Sea of Serenity

Archimedes (crater)

Copernicus (crater)

N

Sea of Storms

Sea of Tranquillity

Kepler (crater)

Sea of Showers

Aristotle (crater)

Sea of Clouds

Tycho (crater)

"Is it beautiful?" Rosie asked.

"It is mostly rocks and dust with no air to breathe and very little gravity," Dad said.

Rosie studied the map some more.

Her dad reached over and pointed at a small crater.

"This crater is named after Copernicus, a famous scientist. Most of the craters are named after famous scientists or philosophers."

Rosie's dad pointed to more craters.

"Here are Plato, Archimedes, Tycho, Kepler, and Aristotle"

"Is there a crater named Rosie?" She asked.

Her dad laughed. "Not yet. When you become a famous scientist, I'm sure they will name one after you."

Moon Word Search

Find the following words in the puzzle:

Atmosphere, Atlas, Basin, Crater, Kepler, Maria, Meteor, Moon, Plato, Space, Tycho

A	T	M	O	S	P	H	E	R	E
R	Y	A	S	Q	R	A	P	O	E
P	C	R	B	E	K	T	J	E	L
M	H	I	T	M	E	L	H	T	P
X	O	A	V	S	P	A	C	E	L
U	R	O	X	F	L	S	Y	M	A
C	V	Q	N	W	E	X	I	P	T
B	A	S	I	N	R	B	J	Y	O

Moon Maze

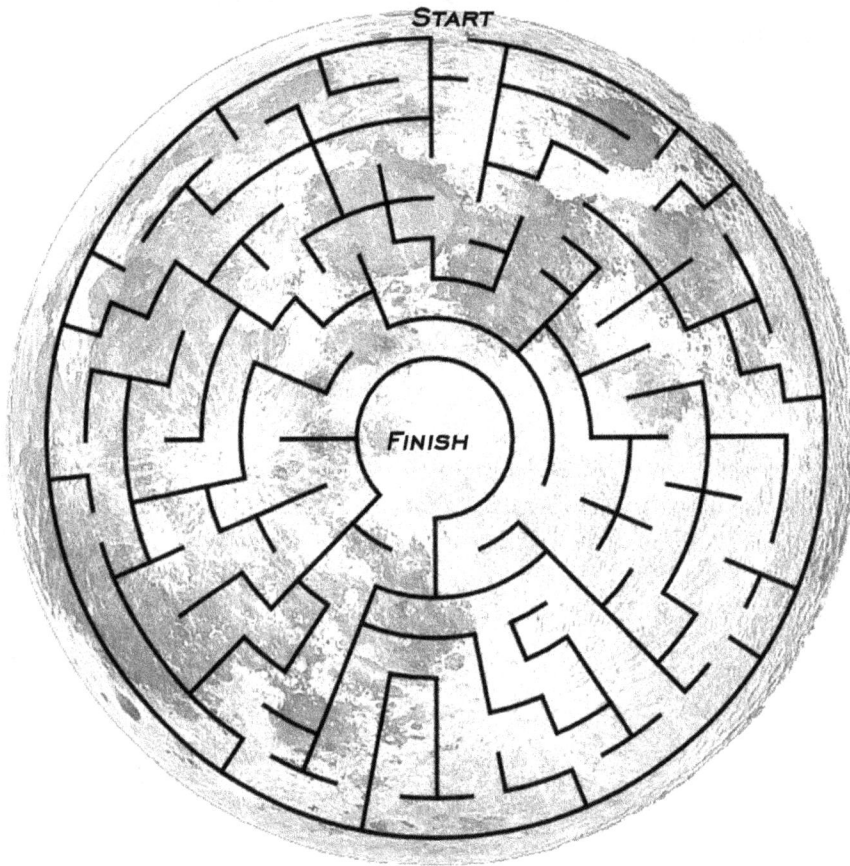

Fill in the blanks with the following words:

rocks, impact basins, lava, Plato, Archimedes, atmosphere, Tycho, Kepler, maria

1. The moon's _____ is too thin to protect it from collisions

   with _____

2. The maria on the moon are _____ _____ filled with _____

3. _____, _____, _____ and _____

   are the names of craters on the moon.

The Moon • Moon Craters

Moon Phases

A couple weeks later, after the dinner dishes were put away. Dad took the family on another walk around the neighborhood.

Rosie looked for the moon, but it was not where she expected it to be. It hung small and thin over the western mountains.

She sulked as she walked.

When they reached home everyone ran inside, eager to get out of the cold.

Rosie sat on the front step and frowned.

"What's wrong?" Dad asked.

"The moon was so small tonight."

"It is a crescent. It looks like the tip of a fingernail doesn't it?"

"How did it change shape so quickly?"

"It didn't actually change shape, it is still a round ball. If you look hard enough you can tell that the rest of the moon is in shadow."

Rosie stared at it for a while. Then she said, "I don't see it."

"Come inside and I will show you a diagram."

Crescent Moon

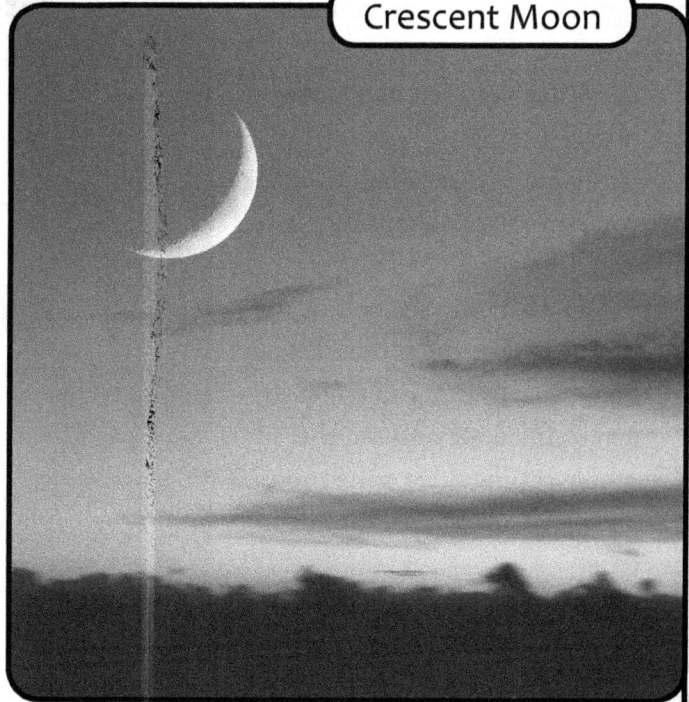

Rosie's dad once again pulled out the space atlas. He opened it to a page that showed a diagram of the moon orbiting the earth.

Rosie looked at the confusing circles. "I don't get it."

"As the moon revolves around the earth, it seems to change shape. But it really stays the same. We see the moon from different angles."

Dad could see she wasn't getting it.

"I'll get your brother to come help," he said.

Dad left the room. He returned with her brother, Michael, a flashlight, and a basketball. He turned off the lights in the room. Then he led Michael to the center of the room.

"I thought you wanted to play ball," Michael complained.

"In a minute. Right now we are going to explain the phases of the moon to your sister."

Michael rolled his eyes.

"You be the sun, son," he said. Then he gave Michael a flashlight. "Shine the light on the ball, no matter when I move."

"You stay on the chair, because it is the earth, Rosie."

He stood behind Michael and held out the ball. "This is the moon."

She giggled, "OK."

"How does the moon look now?"

"Like a ball."

"Good," He moved to the right, a quarter way around the sun.

"What does the ball look like now?"

"I can only see a half of it. Are you standing in the way?" she asked.

"No, you only see half of the bright half of the moon. If you had a space ship, you could fly across from me and see the whole bright side of the moon."

Rosie walked over by the book case.

Phases of the Moon

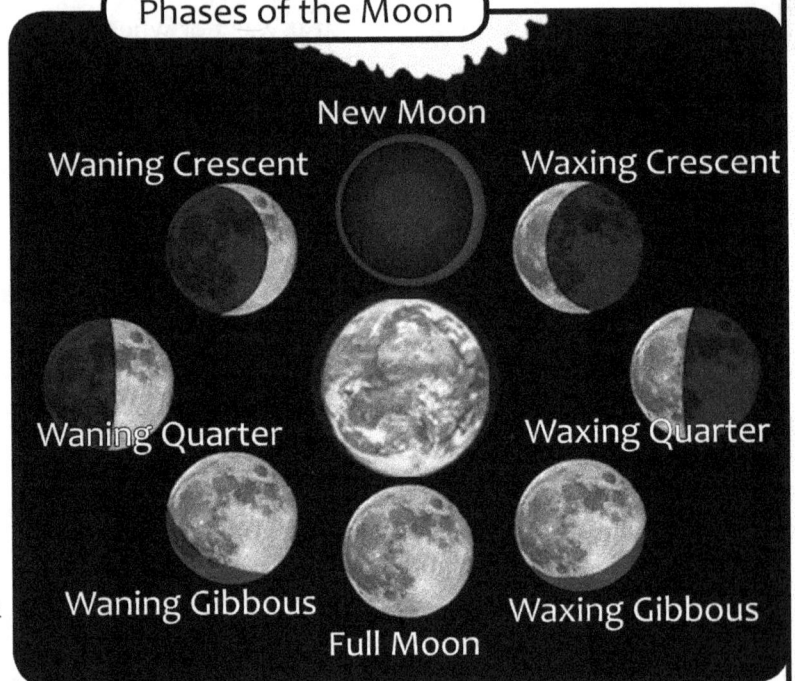

New Moon

Waning Crescent

Waxing Crescent

Waning Quarter

Waxing Quarter

Waning Gibbous

Waxing Gibbous

Full Moon

"I see what you mean."

"Now go back to the earth," Dad said.

Rosie sat down on her original chair. Dad moved another quarter turn around the sun.

"When I put the ball here, what do you see?"

"It is black."

"This is called the new moon, and you can't see it very well. The bright side of the moon is completely away from the earth. This is what the moon will look like in a couple of days. But this evening you saw this."

Rosie's dad moved the ball a few inches to the side.

"Oh, I see. It looks like a crescent now," Rosie said.

"So every time we go on walk in the evening, the moon may look different."

"That is cool."

"It is more than cool," Rosie's dad said. "In ancient times, the shape of the moon kept track of the days and months of the year. Farmers would plant or harvest their crops based on when the full moon was."

"But now we have calendars," Michael said. "The only people who care about full moons are werewolves."

Moon Phase Matching
Match the moon phase with its picture.

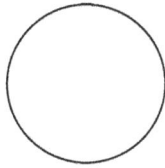

Gibbous

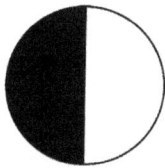

New

Full

Quarter

Crescent

Moon Phases Word Scramble

Unscramble the letters to form words from the story.

BIGUSOB   _____

TESCCNER   _____

ULFL   _____

TAQRREU   _____

ONOM   _____

PILSCEE   _____

Moon

Moon Landing

The family went on a walk the next week. Rosie noticed the gibbous moon in the sky. Her dad threw a tennis ball for the dog to chase.

"Cindy loves to chase balls," Rosie said.

"She sure does."

"I bet she would love to catch the moon sometime."

"I think she would. Too bad it is more than 200,000 miles away."

"That is far. Has anyone ever been there?" Rosie asked.

"Actually, in 1969, men landed on the moon and got to see what it is really like."

"In a space ship like on TV?"

"No, it was on a big rocket. It took three days for them to reach the moon. After they got there, they orbited the moon a few times. Then they sent a lunar lander to the surface. The astronauts explored the moon and collected rock samples for a few hours. Then the astronauts got back on the lander and returned to the main ship which then returned safely back to earth."

"That is cool. I wish I could go to the moon."

They walked in silence for a while. Rosie tripped over a crack in the sidewalk while watching the moon though the trees.

Dad took her hand to steady her.

"Keep focused where you are walking. When we get back to the house I can show you some pictures of the space ship."

Rosie sped by her brother and sister, excited to find out more about a real space ship.

She was already in the den looking at the space atlas when Dad got back.

Dad turned the pages to the section on space flight.

Saturn V Rocket

"This is the Saturn V rocket. It is 363 feet tall. The orbiter and lunar lander are at the very top."

"Did they find any aliens?"

Dad laughed. "The conditions on the moon are too harsh for life to survive. It is either too cold or too hot. There is no atmosphere and 1/6 as much gravity as on the earth."

"How did the astronauts survive?"

"They used special space suits to protect them from the heat and radiation."

"Did they build a moon base?"

"No. Scientists dream of building a moon base one day. But that is a long way off."

"When is the next mission to the moon?"

"NASA hasn't launched a moon mission for long time," Rosie's dad said.

"Are there any more space ships?"

"There are space shuttles, space stations and satellites."

"What are satellites?" Rosie asked.

"They are small unmanned space ships that stay in earth's orbit," Rosie's dad said.

"What are they for?"

"They are very useful. They are used for navigation and television signals. Some are telescopes used to research outer space."

Space Shuttle

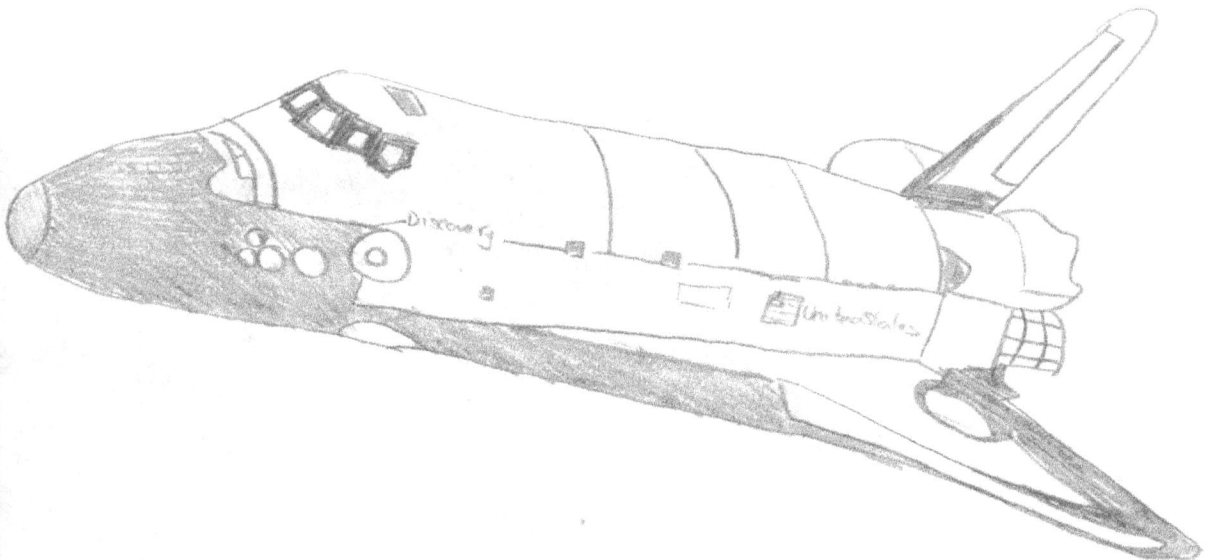

Lunar Code

Use the key to decipher the code.

Key

Special

Harsh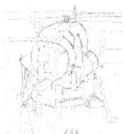

Moon

Used

To Survive

The

Space Suits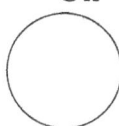

On

Conditions

Astronauts

     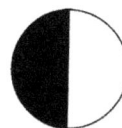

  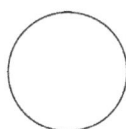  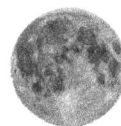

Lunar Landing Hidden Picture

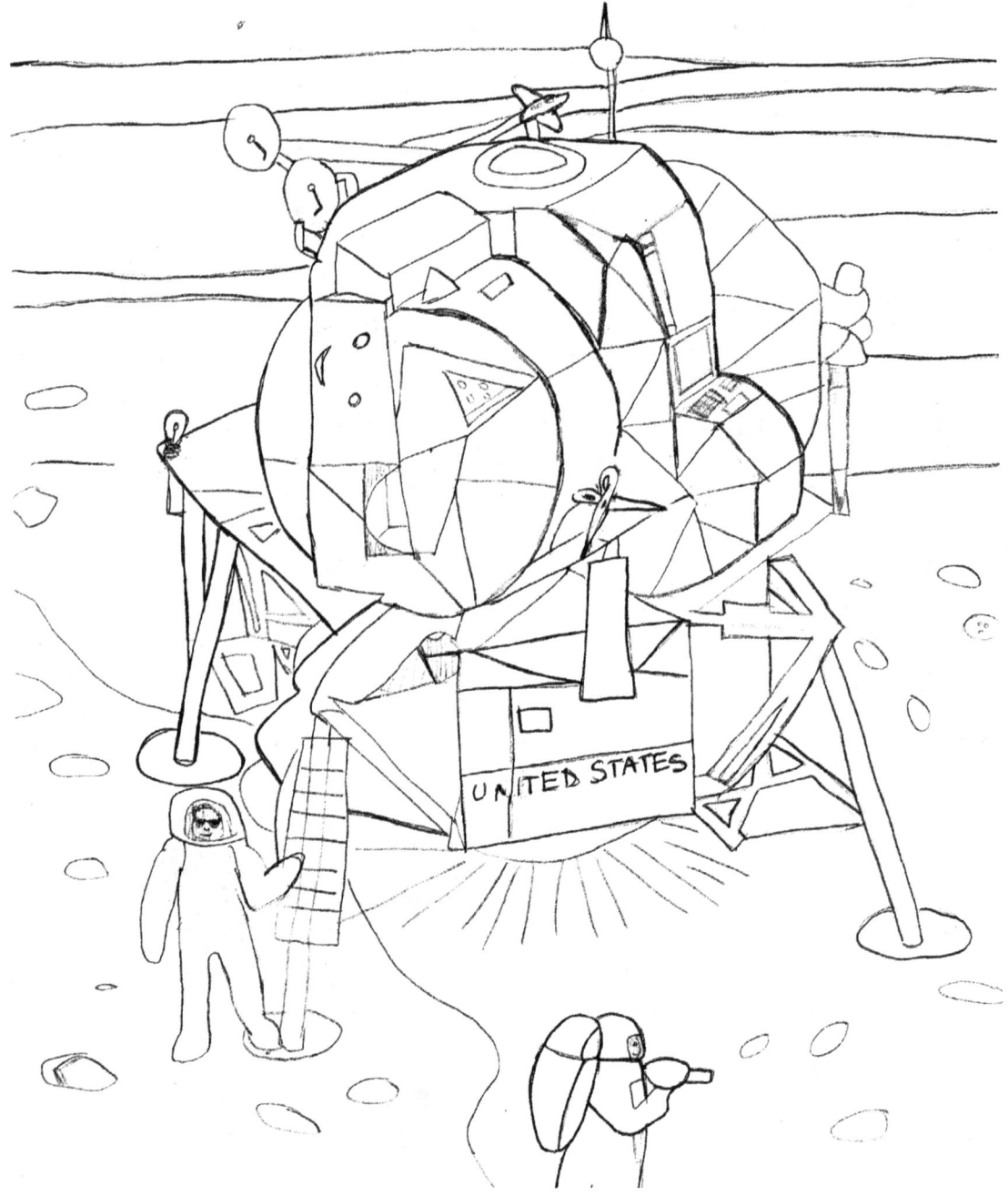

UNITED STATES

airplane	ice cream cone	pencil	smiley face
bowling ball	laptop	pizza	sunglasses
flip-flop	light bulb	scissors	

The Solar System

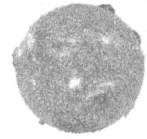

One summer evening, Dad drove the kids to the park. When it started to get late, they got into the car to drive home.

"The sun is in my eyes," Rosie complained.

"At least you aren't driving," Dad said. Then he flipped the front visors down.

"I wish the sun would go behind the mountains."

"You know the sun doesn't go anywhere. It is the earth that turns away from the sun."

"I don't feel the earth moving," Rosie said.

"We don't feel it moving because everything on the earth's surface is moving at the same constant speed. If you close your eyes, do you feel the car moving?"

Rosie closed her eyes.

"No. I feel like I could be sitting on the couch at home. How do scientists know the earth moves?"

"They have measured how the stars appear to move in the sky. That tells them the earth revolves around the sun and the earth spins on its axis. What we see on the earth is the sun moving across the sky."

"I wish I had a diagram," Rosie said.

At the next red light, Rosie's dad reached under his seat. He pulled out a small book and gave it to Rosie.

"Pocket Space Atlas," she read from the cover. Then she smiled and flipped through the pages until she found a diagram of the solar system.

"The people who lived in ancient times believed gods and goddesses ruled the sky. The sun was a god who crossed the sky each day. In the middle ages, astronomers still believed the earth was the center of the

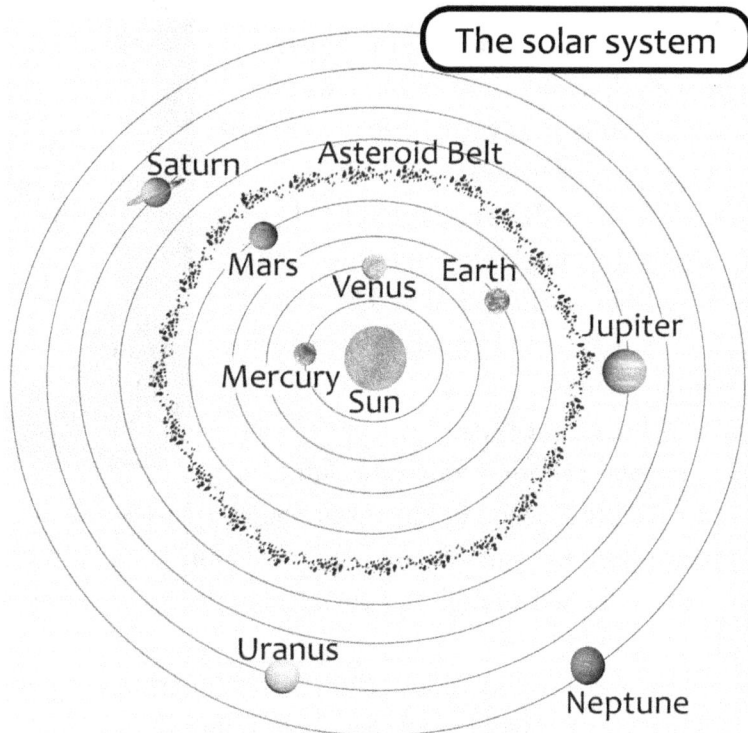

The solar system

Saturn Asteroid Belt
Mars Venus Earth
Mercury Sun Jupiter
Uranus
Neptune

universe."

Rosie read from her pocket space atlas. "The sun is the center of the solar system. The earth is one of the planets that moves around the sun,"

"That's right."

"But the sun looks so small in the sky," Rosie said.

"It is the biggest thing in the solar system by far. See our house down the road? It looks small from here, but when we get closer, it will look much bigger."

"OK"

Rosie watched as their house seemed to grow larger as they got closer.

When they stopped in the driveway, Rosie's dad helped her find a page with a picture of the sun.

"It looks like it is on fire," Rosie said.

"It is. It is a giant nuclear explosion that never ends. The sun is made of hydrogen and helium gases. In the extreme heat and pressure of the sun, those gases give off lots of energy."

"Tomorrow I'm going to go look more closely at the sun," Rosie said.

As they walked toward the house Rosie's dad said, "You must be careful when you look at the sun. It is so bright, it can damage your eyes. You have to look through a special filter." He searched through the junk drawer and pulled out a thick piece of dark glass. "I used this glass to look at the sun during the last eclipse."

"What is an eclipse?"

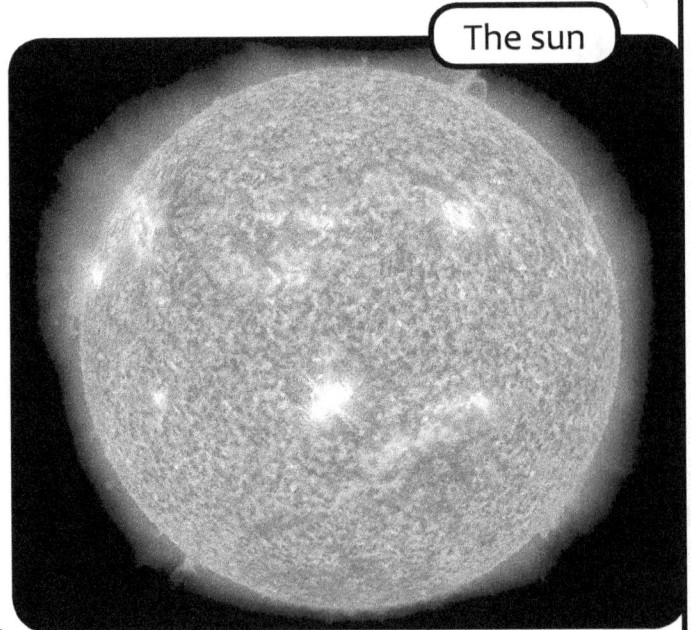
The sun

"A solar eclipse is when the sun is fully or partially blocked by the moon. Solar eclipses only happen about once every 1 and a half years. They are usually only visible on some parts of the earth."

Rosie looked though the dark rectangle and frowned. She couldn't see anything through it.

"The sun is many times brighter than anything in here. If you use that to look at the sun tomorrow, you will see a bright ball of light."

Solar Eclipse Diagram

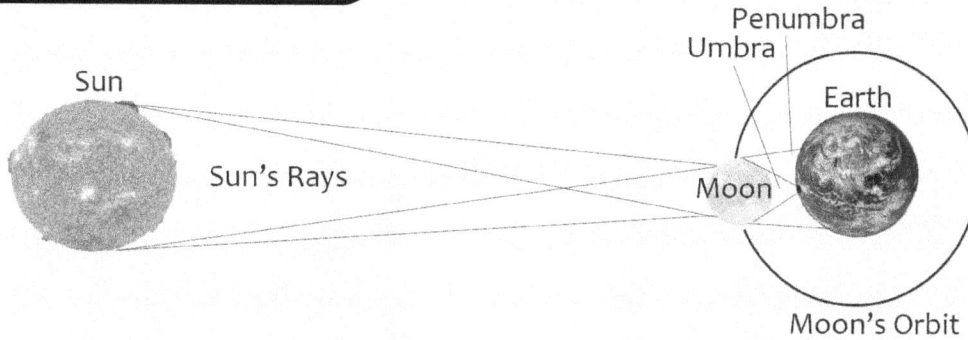

Penumbra
Umbra
Sun
Earth
Sun's Rays
Moon
Moon's Orbit

Sun True/False

____ An eclipse happens only when the sun is completely blocked.

____ Solar eclipses are only visible on some parts of the earth at a time.

____ Solar eclipses happen only during the fall.

____ The Sun is on fire.

____ You don't need to protect your eyes if you look at the sun.

____ The sun has so much energy, you can get sunburned on summer day.

Sun Maze

Start

Finish

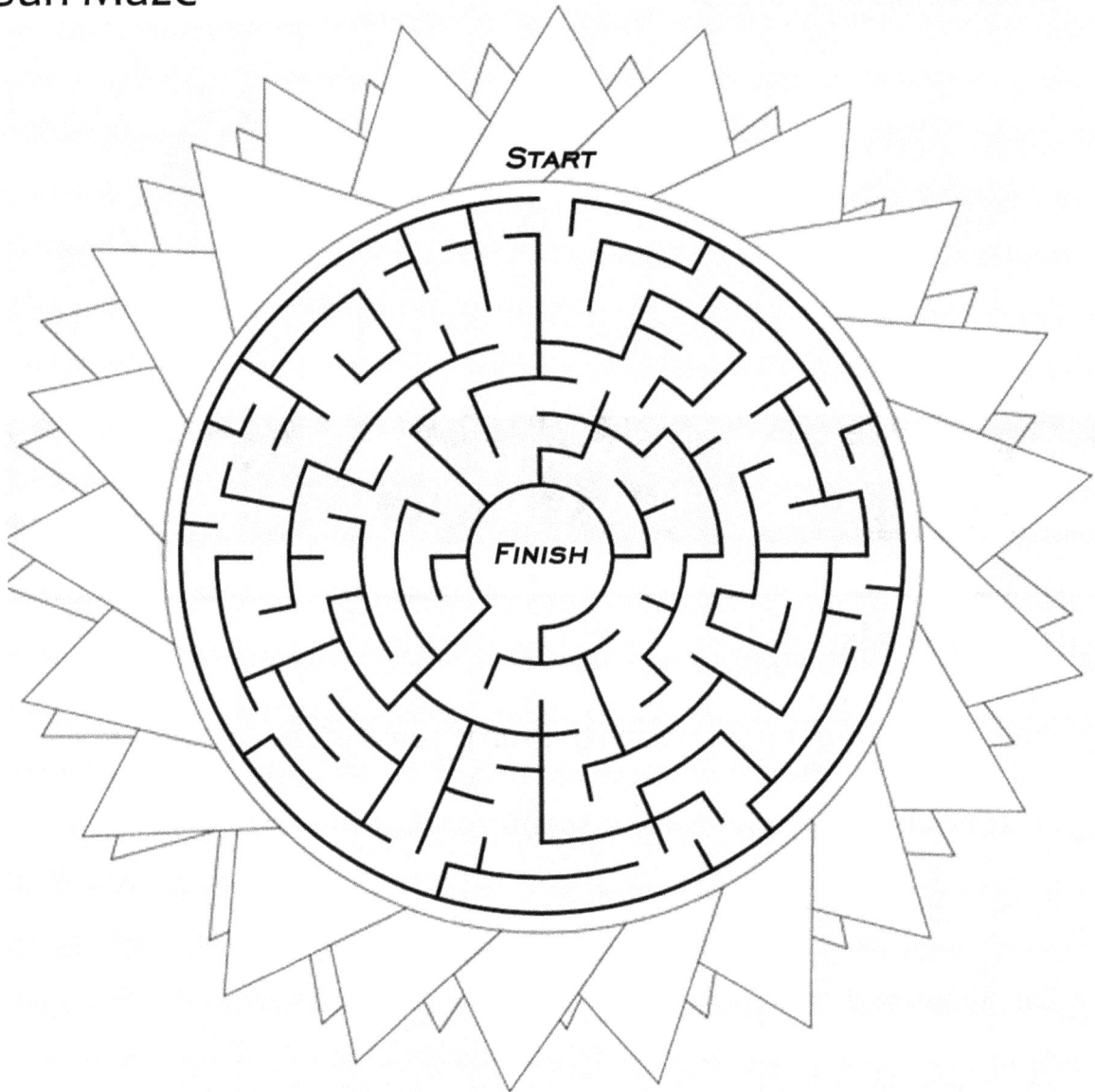

The sun is so _____ you can hurt your eyes if you look at it directly.

The sun is a glowing ball of _____

Solar Flares

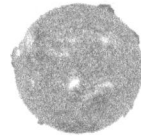

After dinner the next day, Rosie and her dad used the special filter to look at the sun.

"What do you see?" Dad asked Rosie.

"A yellow ball," Rosie said, disappointed.

"That is what you are supposed to see," Dad said.

"I wanted to see rays coming out like in all the pictures."

Dad patted her shoulder.

"Sorry," he said.

"Why do people draw suns with rays?"

"I think they are trying to show the heat that comes from the sun."

Rosie gave the filter back to her dad.

"I'm done with this," she said.

"The sun looks like a ball from earth. But if you have a special telescope, you can see the interesting parts of the sun."

"Do you have one of those telescopes?"

"Sorry, I don't. But you have a space atlas," Dad said.

He opened the atlas to a page that showed a cross-section of the sun.

"The sun is made up of hydrogen and helium gases. These gases burn brightly. But they burn differently in

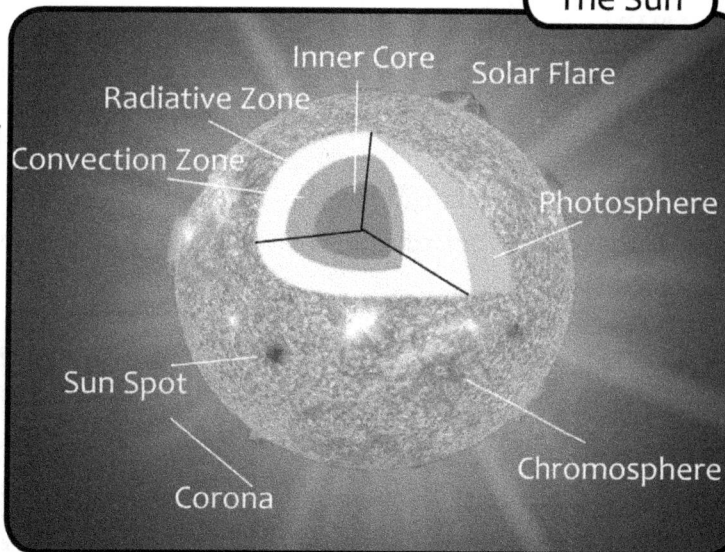

The Sun

different layers of the sun. The deeper they are, the hotter and denser they are," Dad said.

He pointed to the center of the diagram.

"The sun has an inner core. This is where most of the fusion reactions take place."

"What is fusion?"

"Since the sun is so big, the gases are under extreme pressure. Some of the molecules fuse together to form other molecules. That kind of reaction produces a lot heat. Eventually the heat rises outward to the next layer in the sun."

"The radiative zone," Rosie read from the chart.

"Right. The radiative zone is cooler than the core and less dense. Then heat rises to the convective zone. This zone is cooler and less dense than the last layer. Then to the Photosphere."

"Photo like a photograph?" Rosie asked.

"In a way. Photo means light. And most of the light we see is made in the sun's photosphere."

"Is that the last layer?"

"No. Then comes the chromosphere. This layer is actually hotter than the last layer. It is uneven and irregular. It has dips and bumps and makes the sun look like it is on fire."

"So *chromo* means irregular?" Rosie asked.

"No. It means color. This layer has a reddish color. When hydrogen is heated to a specific temperature, it glows red."

"Why doesn't the sun look red then?"

"The red color is mixed with the yellow and white of the sun's corona."

"Corona means crown," Rosie said.

"That's right. The corona looks like a white crown around the sun. You can see it during an eclipse. That is when the bright center of the sun is blocked from view. "

"What are those black spots?"

"Those are sun spots. They look black because they are not as hot as the rest of the sun."

"What is this part?" Rosie asked pointing to a fiery curve coming off the surface of the sun.

"That is a solar flare," Dad said.

"Mom blames solar flares when the internet doesn't work."

Dad laughed.

"They cause interference sometimes," he said.

He turned the page to a picture of the aurora borealis.

"That is so pretty," Rosie said.

"These are caused by solar flares too. So they are not all bad."

I have never seen those outside," Rosie said.

"They are only visible in the far north."

"The sun is cool after all," Rosie said.

aurora borealis

Sun Word Search

Find the following words in the puzzle.

aurora	eclipse	photosphere
bright	filter	radiation
corona	hydrogen	solar flares
degrees	helium	sun spots

```
H  Y  D  R  O  G  E  N  H  S  W
D  E  G  R  E  E  S  O  E  G  I
F  I  L  T  E  R  P  L  L  K  C
X  B  R  I  G  H  T  Q  I  Q  O
E  V  Y  O  U  Y  X  L  U  V  R
C  B  K  O  P  M  S  W  M  S  O
L  F  R  A  D  I  A  T  I  O  N
I  Z  S  T  O  P  S  N  U  S  A
P  H  O  T  O  S  P  H  E  R  E
S  O  L  A  R  F  L  A  R  E  S
E  J  K  T  A  U  R  O  R  A  T
```

Solar Hidden Picture

Find the hidden pictures in the drawing of the sun.

strawberry
toothbrush
bowling ball
pencil
fish

scissors
smiley face
santa hat
baseball bat
pea pod

Seasons

After dinner, Rosie and her family took another walk around the block.

The sun was still up this evening. The breeze was warm and the children did not need any jackets.

"Is the heat in the summer caused by solar flares?" Rosie asked.

"No. Summer heat is affected by the angle of earth's axis of rotation."

"What is an axis of rotation?"

"It is the invisible line through the center of the earth. But the earth's axis is not straight up and down. It is tipped 23.5 degrees."

Her father held up his forearm and leaned it to the side. Then he moved his other arm around it.

"The earth spins like a top around this axis," he said.

Rosie looked confused.

"Do you have your pocket space atlas?" he asked.

Rosie smiled and pulled it out of her back pocket.

They both sat down on the sidewalk to look at it.

She opened to a page that had a diagram of the earth's orbit. It looked like there were four earths in a path around the sun.

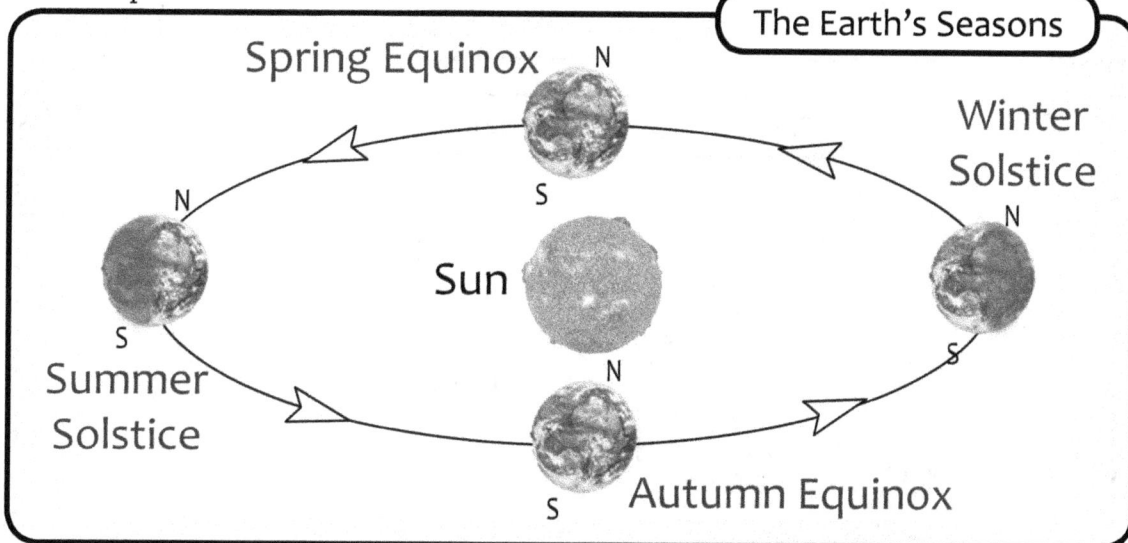

The Earth's Seasons

Spring Equinox
N
S

Winter Solstice
N
S

N
Sun

Summer Solstice
N
S

N
Autumn Equinox
S

"The earth is shaped like a sphere. Half of a sphere is called a hemisphere," he explained.

"We live in the northern hemisphere. When our side of the earth is tipped toward the sun, we get summer. Why do you think?"

"Because we are closer to the sun," Rosie said.

"There is much more to it than that."

Dad picked up a round rock from their neighbor's landscaping. Then he took his pen light out of his pocket. He marked a spot on the rock with the pen.

"Hold the light while I spin the rock."

Rosie held the light.

"This spot is in the northern hemisphere. It is tipped toward the light in summer. It gets more sunlight in a day. And the rays hit the spot more directly."

Dad rotated the rock to demonstrate.

"Then in winter, the days are shorter and the sun is at an angle."

This time Dad tipped the mark away from the light.

"OK, What about spring and fall?"

"In spring or fall, the length of the day and the night is almost equal. When they are exactly equal it is called an equinox."

"The days that are the shortest or longest of the year are called solstices."

Rosie nodded as if she understood.

"Is it summer everywhere at the same time?"

"No. When it is summer here, it is winter in the southern hemisphere. If our side of the earth points toward the sun, the other side is pointing away."

"I wish we could always have summer," Rosie said.

"Seasons are important. The uneven heating keeps the air moving. Snow and storms are not fun, but they mix up the air. They bring water for drinking. They help crops grow. If we had summer all the time, it would soon be too hot for us to live."

Direct and Indirect Solar Radiation

Indirect Rays

Direct Rays

Seasons Word Scramble
Unscramble the words and then fill in the blanks.

XSIA   _____

SAONSSE   _____

NITWRE   _____

PONSXUREE _____

NOXIUQE   _____

TICELOSS   _____

MUSREM   _____

The earth's _____ is tipped 23.5 degrees.

In the _____ the earth gets more _____ from the sun.

An _____ is when the length of the day and the length of the night are equal.

When it is _____ in the southern hemisphere it is _____ in the northern hemisphere.

The tilt of earth's axis causes _____.

Seasons Coloring Page

The earth has seasons because it spins on a tipped _____

Classification

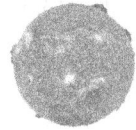

Rosie and her dad were waiting in line at the grocery store. She saw a magazine with fancy people on it.

"Why do they call these people stars?" she asked her dad.

"People admire them. They are beautiful and successful. They call them stars because they seem brighter than the rest of us," he answered.

"Do they glow?" Rosie asked.

Rosie's dad chuckled. "No, they are just people."

"I thought all the stars were very far away," Rosie said.

"Most of them are farther than you can imagine. But one is very close, our sun."

"I thought they were just little points of light in the sky."

"No. They are burning hot balls of gas. Our sun is one of them," Dad said.

"How do they know how far away a star is?" Rosie asked.

"If the star is close enough, astronomers use parallax."

"Pair of what?" Rosie asked.

"Parallax is using angles to measure how far away a star is."

Rosie's dad pointed the penlight at Rosie.

"Cover one eye and then the other," he told her.

Rosie did. Then she asked, "Did you move the light?"

"No. Each eye sees the penlight from a different angle. That makes it seem like the pen moved. Stars that are not too far away can be measured this way. Astronomers have to use points that are much farther away than two eyes."

"Do they use two telescopes on different sides of the earth?"

"They need to be farther away than that. They take measurements 6 months apart. Then the measurements are on opposite ends

Parallax diagram

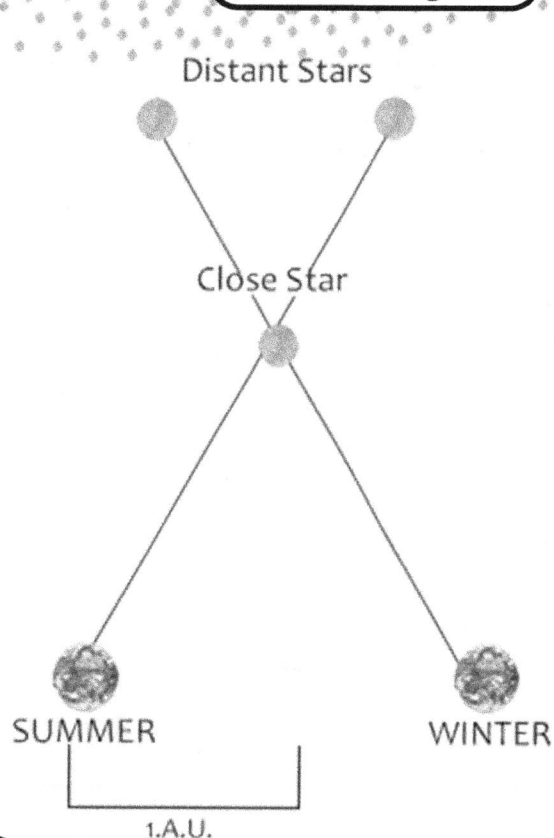

Distant Stars

Close Star

SUMMER

WINTER

1.A.U.

of the earth's orbit."

"That is cool."

"When stars are too far away, parallax doesn't work. Astronomers use other kinds of information to help them measure the most distant stars.

"What kind of information?"

"They need to measure their brightness and color. Then they can estimate the distance bases on what they have learned from stars they can measure with parallax. "

"Aren't all stars yellow?"

"There were many types of stars. Red giants, blue supergiants and brown dwarfs for example. Do you have your pocket space atlas?"

Rosie took her atlas out of her purse.

"Red giants are 100 to 1000 times the size of our sun. Blue supergiant stars are about 25 times the size our sun, but are much hotter than the red stars. Brown dwarf stars are smaller than our sun. A star may become a supernova or even a black hole when they get really old."

"What kind of star is our sun?"

"It is an average or main sequence star," Dad added.

"Oh, I was hoping our star would be special," Rosie said.

"Average is good. That means it is stable. We will be able to depend on our sun for many years to come."

Classification of Stars

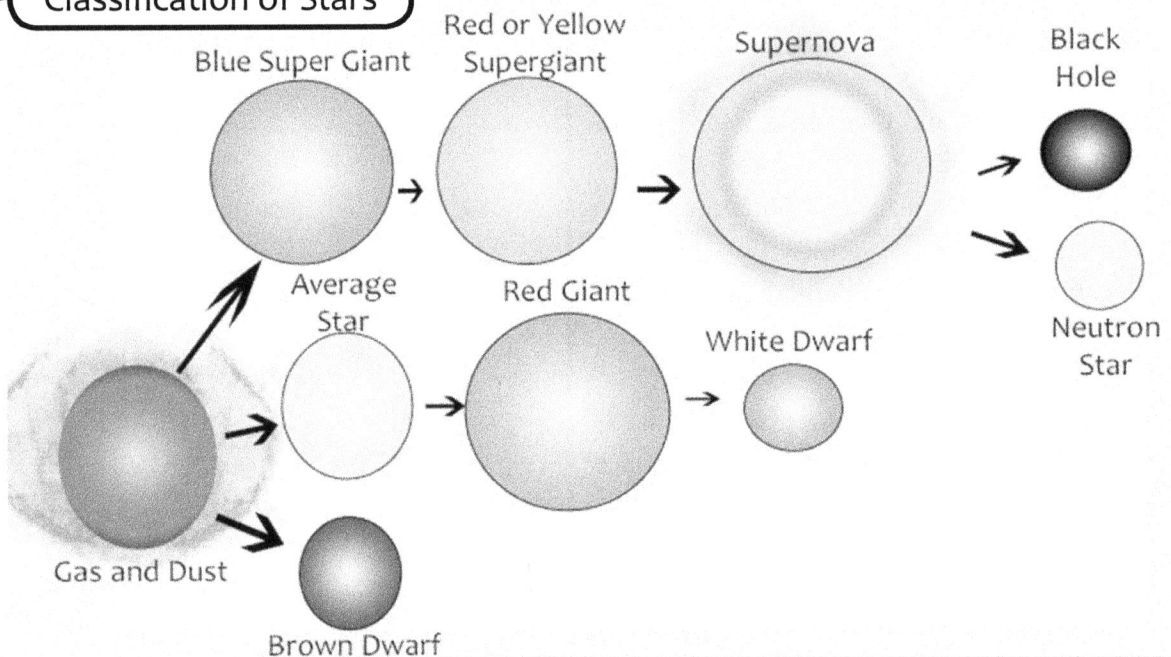

Blue Super Giant

Red or Yellow Supergiant

Supernova

Black Hole

Average Star

Red Giant

White Dwarf

Neutron Star

Gas and Dust

Brown Dwarf

Star Word Search

```
A  H  Q  B  D  L  I  G  H  T
V  Y  F  L  W  X  R  A  Y  H
O  D  Z  A  A  O  V  K  B  G
N  R  S  C  R  I  L  L  O  I
R  O  V  K  F  D  Z  L  X  R
E  G  X  H  S  A  E  B  E  B
P  E  Q  O  T  R  A  T  S  Y
U  N  K  L  A  X  Z  P  Y  K
S  U  P  E  R  G  I  A  N  T
```

star
light
bright
yellow

hydrogen
supergiant
dwarf star
supernova

black hole
radio
xray

Circle the one that is bigger:

White dwarf **or** average star

Super nova **or** black hole

blue supergiant **or** supernova

neutron star **or** red giant

earth **or** sun

brown dwarf **or** average star

Star Classification True/False

___Something that is brighter is always closer.

___There are many stars in the universe.

___All small bright objects in the sky are stars.

___Light pollution makes seeing stars harder in the city.

___The sun uses hydrogen to make energy

___Scientists know what stars are like because they have space ships.

___A red supergiant star could become a black hole.

Pleiades Star Cluster

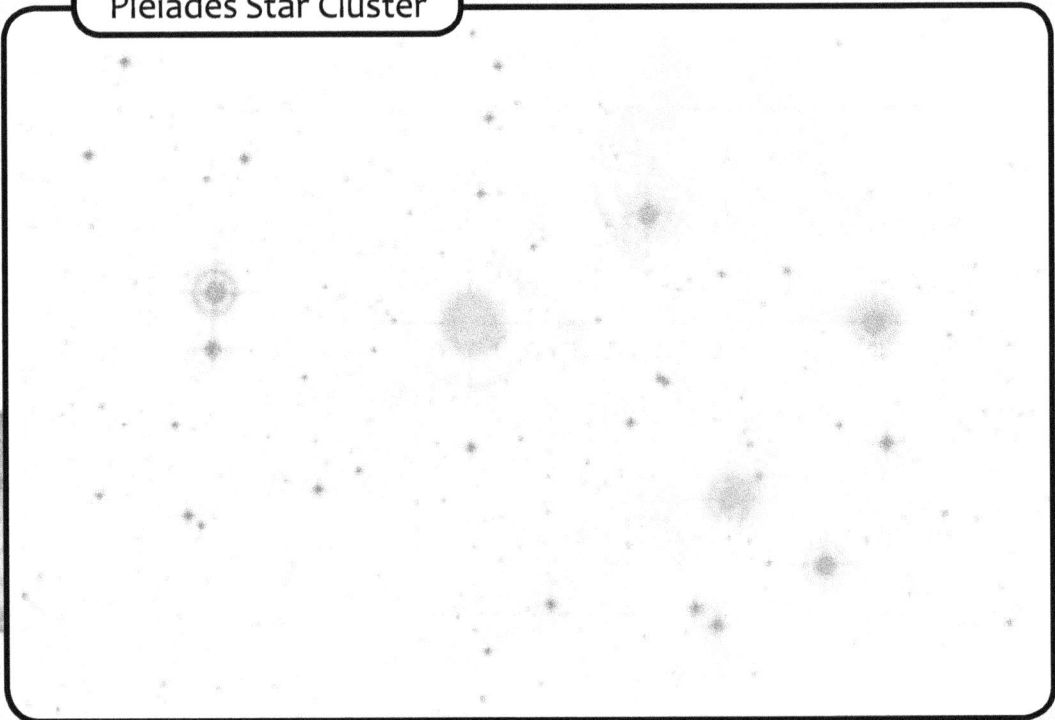

Constellations

Rosie's dad took the family camping.

"Nothing like clean, mountain air," he told the kids.

They ate hot dogs and marshmallows around the campfire as the sky grew dark.

When they got tired, they unrolled their sleeping bags.

Rosie looked up at the night sky. There were so many stars it made her dizzy.

"There must be more stars in the mountains," she said.

"It seems that way," her dad answered.

"I won't be able to sleep. The stars are too bright," Rosie said.

"In ancient times, people saw pictures in the sky and told stories about them."

"I don't see any pictures," Rosie said.

"You have to connect the dots," Dad said.

"And use a lot of imagination," Michael added from across the campfire.

"Star pictures are called constellations or signs. They represent heroes and monsters of ancient myths," Dad said.

"Do you know any of the stories?" Rosie asked.

"Sagittarius is in the southern sky. The Greeks said it was a centaur shooting an arrow," Dad said pointing to the south.

"That looks more like a teapot," Michael said.

"Use your imagination."

"I think I can see it," Rosie said.

"Sagittarius is aiming his bow at Scorpius. Scorpius looks like a big letter 'J'."

"The 'J' could be the scorpion's tail," Rosie said.

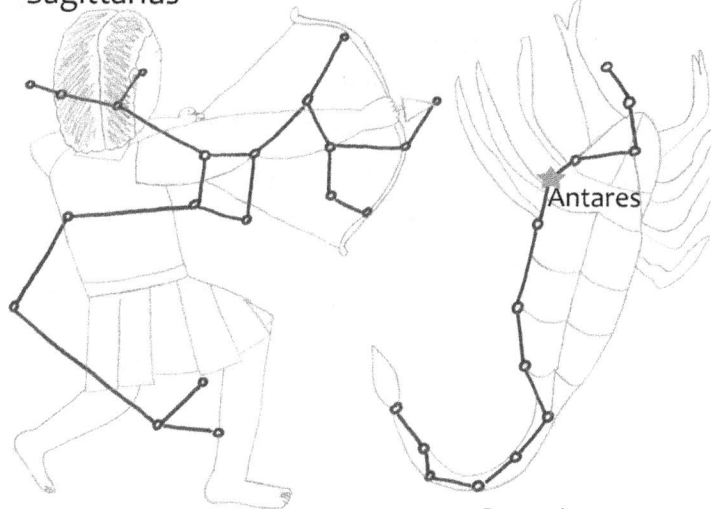

Sagittarius

Antares

Scorpius

"Antares is a red star in the heart of the scorpion. It is one of the brightest stars in the sky," Dad said.

"Tell her about the Zodiac, Dad," Rosie's brother said.

"Zodiac comes from a Latin word that means circle of animals."

"Except they are not all animals," her brother added.

Dad sighed. "Most of them are animals. The zodiac constellations circle the earth on the ecliptic."

"What is an ecliptic?"

"It is an imaginary circle around the sky near the horizon. The sun appears to move along this circle during the year."

"The sun doesn't move, the earth does," Michael said.

"I said it appears to move. It looks like it moves compared to the stars in the background."

"OK," Michael said, turning over in his sleeping bag.

"Many ancient cultures believe the location of the sun in the zodiac it important. Everyone gets a zodiac sign depending on when they were born."

"Do I have a Zodiac sign?"

"You were born in early March, so you are a Pisces."

"How do they know which sign the sun is in when it is light outside?" Michael asked.

"Astronomers know which signs are opposite," Dad explained. "Just because they lived a long time ago, doesn't make them dumb."

Michael chuckled.

"There are other constellations outside the ecliptic. Some are seasonal like Orion. Some constellations are polar, or high in the sky. The big dipper is a polar constellation. It is visible all year long."

"I have seen the big dipper before," Rosie said.

"If you follow the line of the dipper's cup it will point to the North Star. The North Star is almost exactly north. Sailors used it to find their way at night."

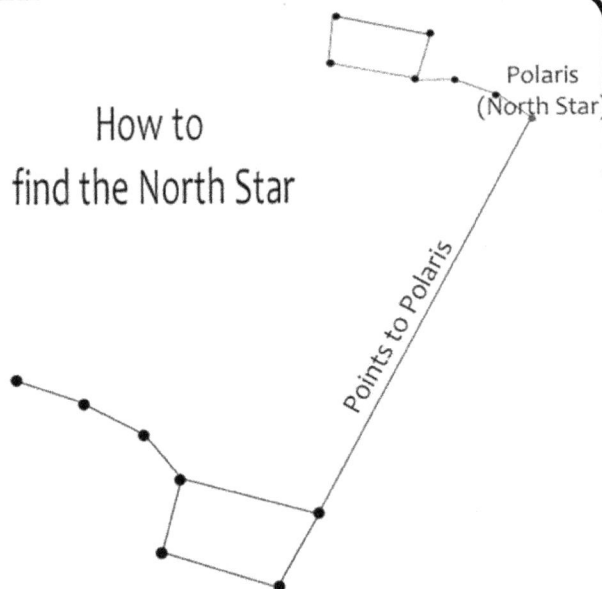

How to find the North Star

Polaris (North Star)

Points to Polaris

Star Constellation Code

Use the key to decipher the code.

♌ – of stars	♍ – in the
♏ – The zodiac	♊ – are
♓ – ecliptic	♑ – group
♉ – constellations	♈ – night
♋ – groups	♒ – of
♎ – sky	♐ – is a

♉   ♊   ♋   ♌   ♍   ♈   ♎ .

_____

♏   ♐   ♑   ♒   ♉   ♍   ♓

_____

Signs of the Zodiac

Constellation dot-to-dot

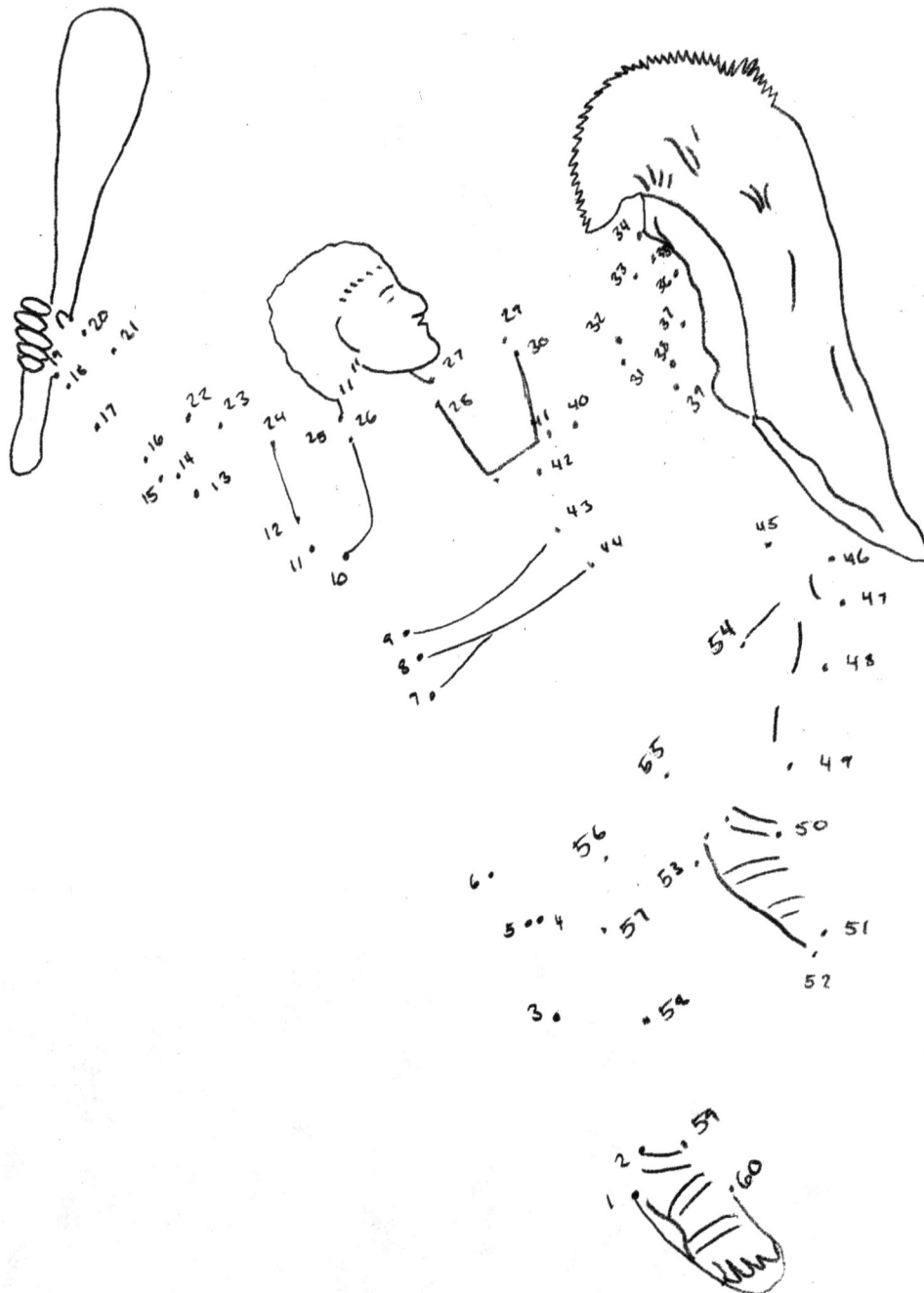

Galaxies

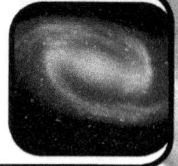

After hiking all day, the tired children crawled into their sleeping bags.
Rosie stared at the clear night sky.

"There is a strange cloud in the middle of the stars," she said.

"There are no clouds tonight," Dad said.

"Part of the sky looks white over there."

"That is the Milky Way. The ancients thought it looked like spilled milk in the sky. But now we know that is part of our galaxy."

"What is a galaxy?"

"A galaxy is a collection of stars, gases, and space dust. Earth is in a galaxy called the Milky Way. You can see part of it in the sky."

"Are all the stars in the Milky Way?"

"All the stars we can see with the naked eye are in the Milky Way. But many more are not. Astronomers have found countless galaxies. At first they thought they looked like smudged stars or clouds. But with modern telescopes we can tell the smudges are groups of stars."

"What does our galaxy look like?" Rosie asked.

"The Milky Way is a spiral galaxy. That white streak you see in the sky is one of the spiral's arms."

"Are all the galaxies shaped like spirals?" she asked.

"No. Some galaxies are shaped like balls. Others may have an egg shape. Still others may be barred spirals."

"How do they know there are so many galaxies? They are so far away it takes billions of years for their light to reach the earth," Michael said from his sleeping bag.

"Even if the light is billions of years old, we can still see it."

"How do they see it?" Rosie asked.

"Scientist use different kinds of telescopes. Telescopes can measure more than visible light. They also measure radio and x-ray emissions. Space telescopes can get more detailed

The Milky Way Galaxy

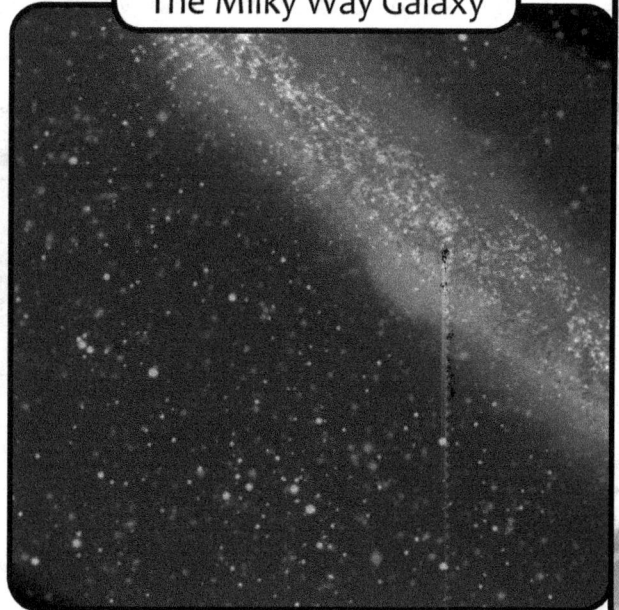

pictures. They don't have to see through the earth's atmosphere."

"How do astronomers know what the milky way looks like if we are inside of it?"

"You are inside your body. How do you know what your arm looks like?"

Rosie held up her hand and looked at it.

"The Milky Way Galaxy has many arms that we can see from earth," Dad said.

"Arms like a spider?" she asked.

"Not like a spider, like a spiral. It has a bright center that scientists call a bulge. It has lots of old red and yellow stars so it looks orange."

Dad sat down by Rosie. He showed her his cup of hot cocoa.

"Since you don't have your atlas, I have something that looks like the Milky Way."

Rosie's dad put a small marshmallow in the center of his cup. Then he took a spoon and slowly stirred it as it melted.

"This is like the Milky Way. It has a big center with curved arms."

"That is cool. Can I have Milky Way cocoa before I go to sleep too?"

Milky Way Galaxy Map

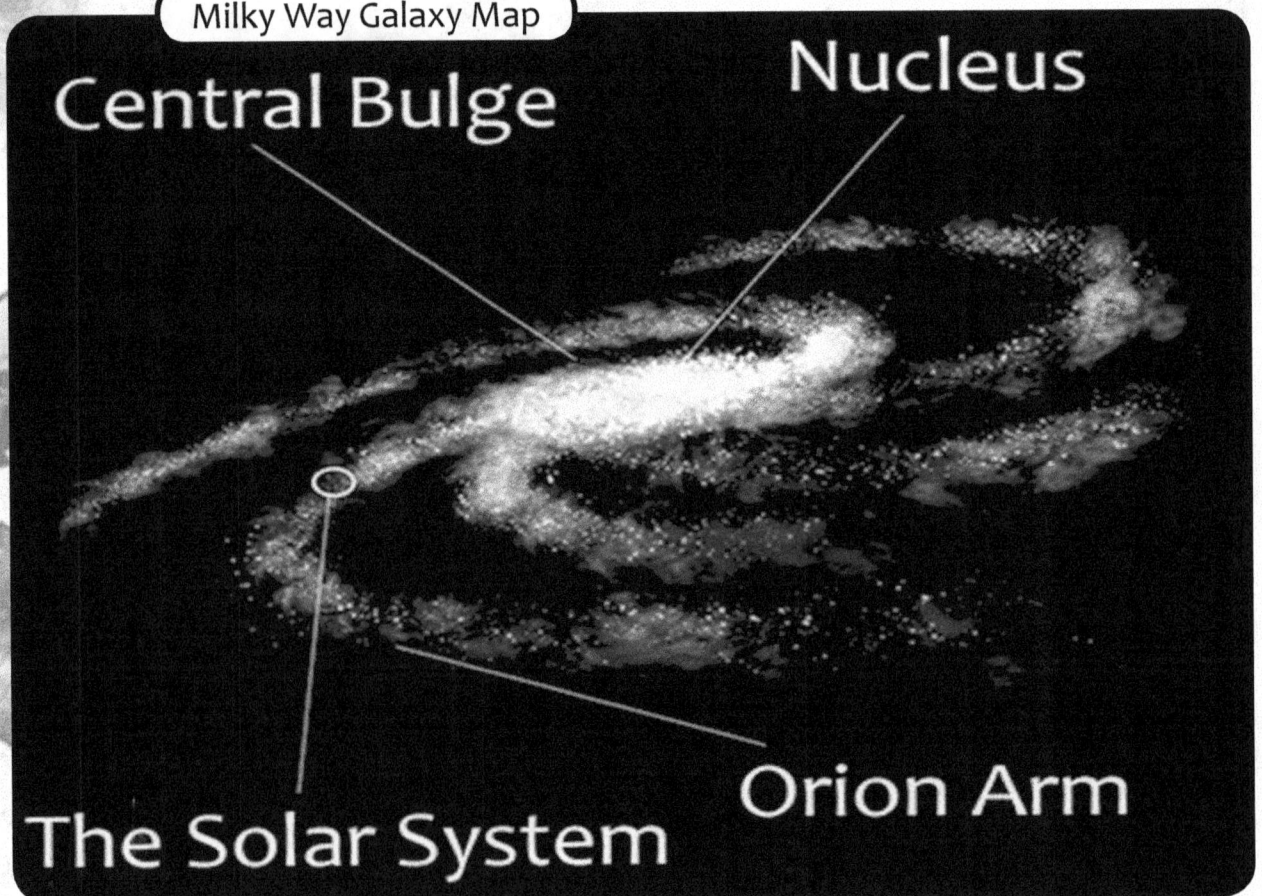

Central Bulge

Nucleus

The Solar System

Orion Arm

Galaxy Matching

Spiral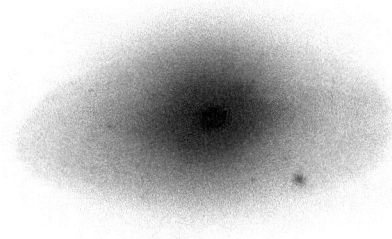

Bar-Spiral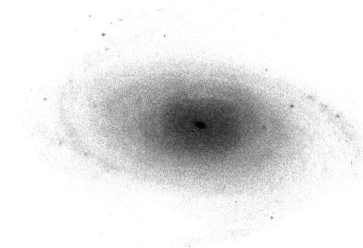

Elliptical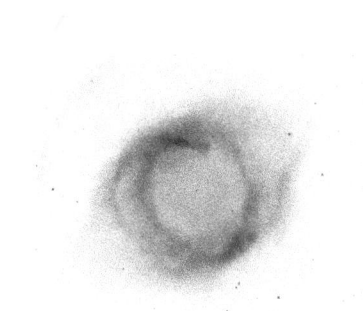

Irregular

Galaxy Maze

START

FINISH

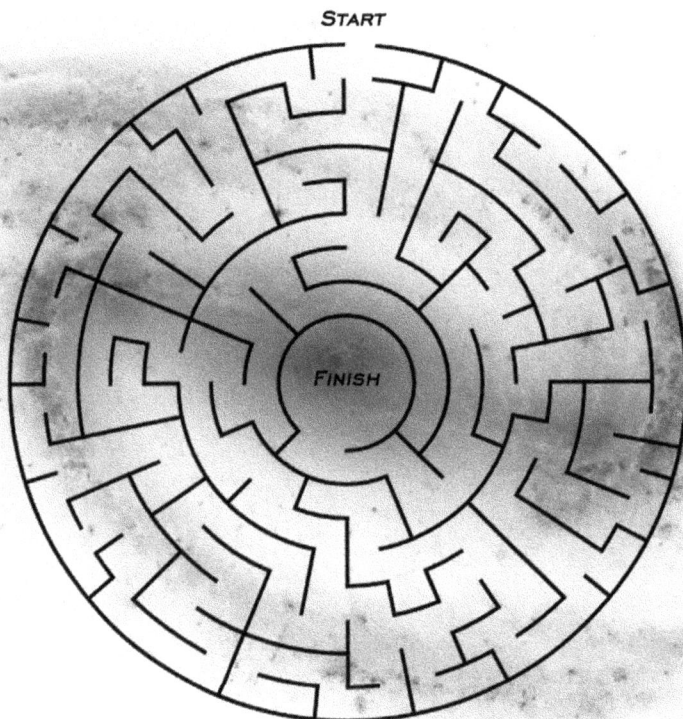

Galaxies are groups of stars. Our galaxy is called the

_____ _____

Mercury

The family drove through the desert on their way to a beach vacation. They had to stop to get gas during the hot afternoon.

Dad made the kids get out to stretch their legs.

"This is the hottest place in the universe," Rosie's older sister, Jane, said. She stood in a small patch of shade near the gas pump.

"The sun is hotter than this," Rosie said.

"A blue super giant star is even hotter than that," Michael added.

"I know we are not standing on a star," Jane said. "This is the hottest place on any planet in the universe."

"Do you mean universe or solar system?" Michael asked.

"You are so frustrating," Jane said.

"Mercury must be the hottest planet. It is the closest to the sun," Rosie said.

"Venus is hotter. Haven't you heard of the green-house effect?" Michael said.

Rosie's dad opened the car door.

"That's enough. Do you want to stand in this heat all day?"

They stopped arguing and climbed in the car.

Surface of Mercury

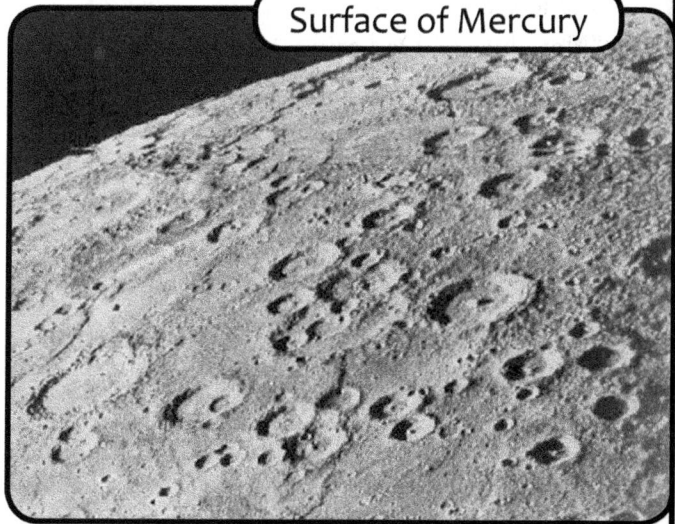

"Mercury is not the hottest, but it gets the most solar radiation." Dad said. He shaded his eyes against the sun.

Then he got in the car and cranked the air conditioning.

"How much longer until we get to the beach?" Jane asked.

"Only a few more hours," dad said.

The kids groaned.

"We have been in the car all day," Jane said.

"A day on Mercury is 58 earth-days? At least we haven't been driving that long," Michael said.

"Why is Mercury's day so long?" Rosie asked.

"The sun's gravity slows down Mercury's rotation."

"Does it have a slow year too?" she asked.

"It's year is 88 earth days. If you were born on Mercury, you would be 41-years-old."

Rosie giggled.

"Mercury is almost the same size as the moon," Rosie said.

"But it is more dense," Dad said.

"It has an iron core which makes it heavy for its size." Rosie added.

"Are you reading from your pocket space atlas?" Michael accused.

"It has small craters because it has strong gravity," she added.

Michael snatched the atlas away.

"No reading in the car, it will make you sick," Jane said, "Remember last time?"

Rosie huffed.

"Can you see Mercury in the sky?" Rosie asked.

"Not always," Dad said.

"That's because sometimes it is behind the sun," Michael said.

"Right. If you do see Mercury, it will be low in the sky at dawn or dusk."

"Why is it so low in the sky?"

"It is near the horizon because it is so close to the sun. When the sun rises or sets, Mercury rises or sets soon after."

The earth, the moon and Mercury

Earth

Mercury

The Moon

Planets in the night sky

Saturn

Venus

Mercury

The Inner Planets • Mercury

Mercury Word Fill-in

Use the words in the box to fill in the blanks below.

Mercury	iron	58
gravity	88	craters
radiation	sun	

Mercury has a large _____ core that makes it heavy for its small size

It receives the most solar _____

Scientists can tell Mercury has strong _____

because it has small _____

A day on Mercury is _____ earth-days. A Mercury year is _____ earth-days.

Mercury is the first planet from the _____.

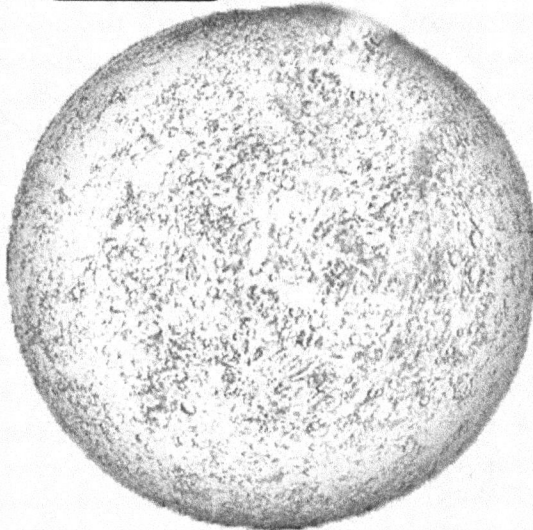

Mercury

Mercury Maze

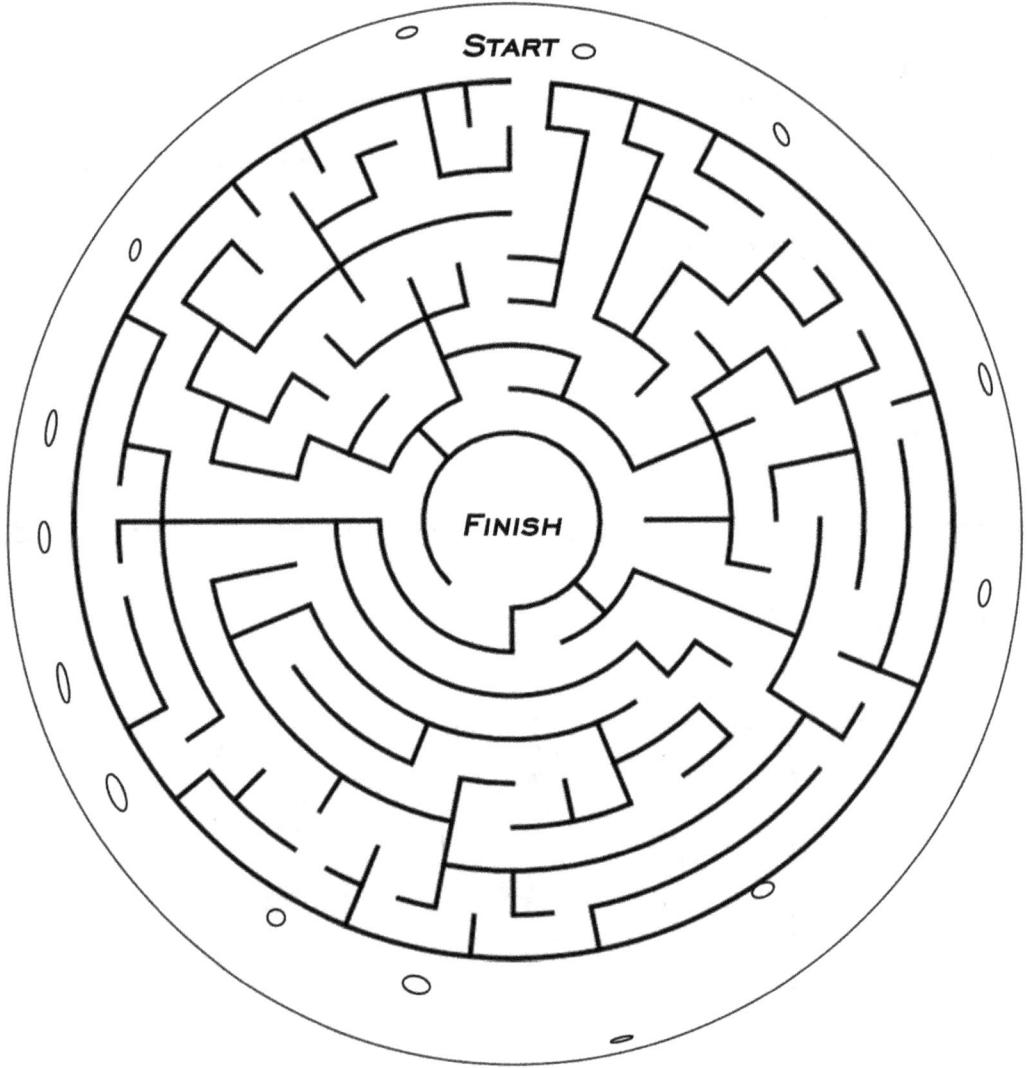

START ○

FINISH

Venus

Dad and the kids walked through rows of plants in a greenhouse.

"Why are we here?" Jane asked.

"We are picking tomatoes," Dad explained.

"Then why are we walking by all these plants?" Michael asked.

"The ripe fruit is in the back. We need the reddest, ripest fruit."

"It is so hot," Jane said.

"We are in a greenhouse," Michael said. "Of course it is hot."

"But the roof is only plastic," Rosie said.

"The plastic roof keeps sun-warmed air from escaping," Dad said.

Greenhouse

"Venus has a greenhouse effect. That's why it is the hottest planet in the solar system," Michael said.

"But it isn't covered in plastic," Rosie said.

"No, it is covered in carbon dioxide gas," Michael said.

"Carbon dioxide acts like a plastic roof. It absorbs the sun's heat, but won't let it escape back into space," Rosie's dad explained.

"It gets so hot on Venus that lead melts," Michael said.

Rosie's eyes went wide.

When they reached the back of the greenhouse, they filled their baskets with tomatoes.

"These are too heavy for me," Rosie said. She handed her basket to Michael.

"It is not as heavy as the air on Venus," Dad said.

"What do you mean?"

"The atmosphere is very dense. It is about 90 times heavier than earth's atmosphere," Dad said.

"If you went to Venus, you would be crushed like a bug," Michael cackled. Then he picked up an ant with his fingers and smashed it.

"That's enough," Dad said as he pulled Michael along.

Rosie followed behind them. She looked for Venus in her pocket space atlas.

"My atlas says Venus is the most like earth," Rosie said.

"It is close to the same size, mass and position. But they are very different worlds," Dad said.

"They both have clouds," Rosie said.

"Venus has rain clouds made of sulfuric acid," Michael said.

"That's right. And the rest of the atmosphere is so thick, we can't see the surface with telescopes."

"What about radar?" Michael asked.

"Radar is not that helpful. It wasn't until scientists sent probes to Venus in the 1960's that we had any idea what the surface of Venus was like."

"What is it like?" Rosie asked.

"It is a barren, rocky world. Most of its surface is covered with volcanic rock," Dad said.

"It says here that Venus' day is longer than its year," Rosie read.

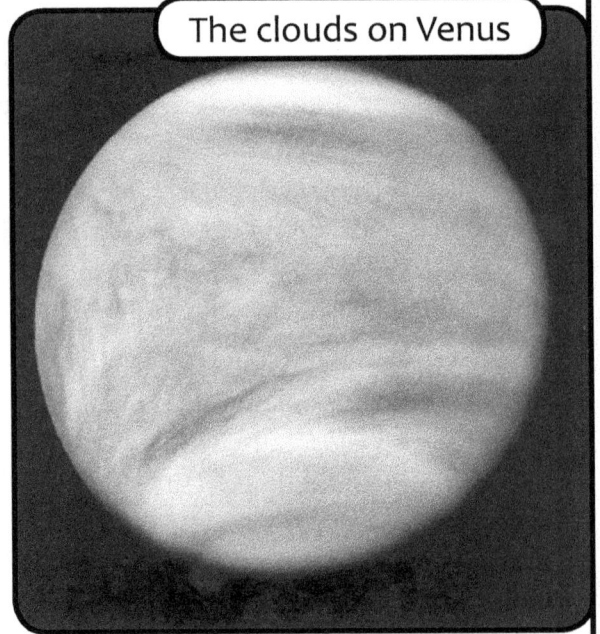

The clouds on Venus

"Even with such long days and nights, the temperature on Venus doesn't change much. The thick clouds shield Venus from the sun."

Dad led the children to the front of the greenhouse to pay for the tomatoes.

"Venus is the third brightest object in the sky after the sun and the moon."

"If you look at Venus through a telescope, you will see it change shape like the moon does," Dad said.

"I can't wait to look for it."

"I can't wait to get out of this hot house," Michael said.

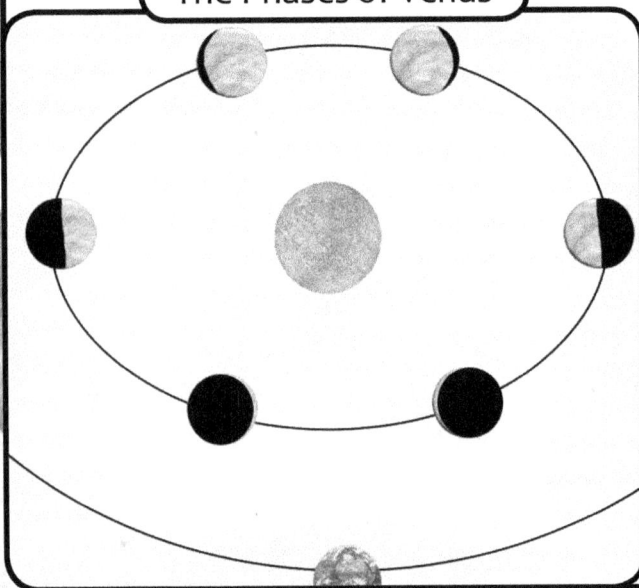

The Phases of Venus

The Inner Planets • Venus

Venus Code

Use the key to decode the sentence.

Key				
☉	☽	☿	⊕	♃
in	hottest	greenhouse	Venus	planet
♂	♀	♆	♄	♅
system	makes	the	effect	solar

♆ ☿ ♄ ♀ ⊕

___

♆ ☽ ♃ ☉ ♆ ♅ ♂

___

The Inner Planets • Venus

Venus True/False

___Venus' atmosphere is almost all carbon dioxide.

___There are many pictures of the surface of Venus.

___Venus is warmer than Mercury.

___Venus is the third planet from the sun.

___Any spacecraft sent to the surface of Venus is quickly melted or corroded.

___Venus' day is longer than its year.

Venus

Mars

One night, the kids watched a movie about Martians invading the Earth.

Rosie hid under her blanket. She couldn't bear to watch the aliens take over the planet.

"Mars is a cold, dead world," she said. "Martians are not real."

"Mars is a lot like Earth. Its day is 25 hours long. It has seasons," Dad said.

"Some parts of Canada can be colder than Mars in the winter," Michael said smiling.

"Those parts of Canada are frozen wastelands," Rosie said.

"All you need for life to exist is water," Michael said.

"The water on Mars is frozen," Rosie said.

"Scientists have seen canals there."

"They aren't real canals, just odd surface features. Satellites take pictures of Mars all the time. They have never seen any evidence of life."

"Maybe the Martians are underground where the satellites can't see them," Michael said.

Rosie huddled deeper in her blanket.

"Are you saying Martians could really take over the earth?" she asked shakily.

"They haven't found any life on Mars," Rosie's dad said, patting her shoulder.

Rosie sighed in relief.

"Is there water on Mars?" she asked.

"No liquid water. It is either frozen or vaporized in the thin atmosphere," her dad said.

"Scientists think Mars had liquid water a long time ago. That was when the Martians thrived," Michael said.

"Mars has polar ice like earth. These ice caps are made of water-ice and frozen carbon dioxide. They change size as the seasons change just like earth's ice caps do," Dad said.

"When that ice melts, the Martians will wake up and take over the earth," Michael said.

"What?" Rosie asked.

Rosie's eyes got large.

"There are no Martians," Dad said.

"Are you sure?" Michael asked. "Has anyone been there?"

Polar ice cap on Mars.

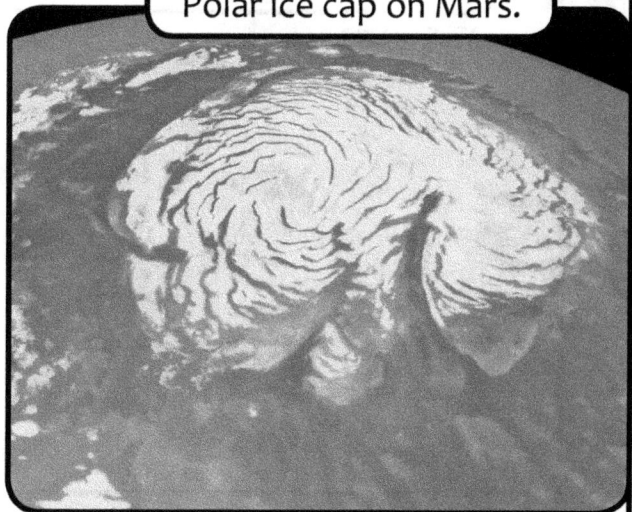

"Scientists have sent probes and rovers to Mars. A few of them are still there studying the surface with special instruments."

Dad took the space atlas and turned to a page of a rocky, red landscape.

"Everything looks red," Rosie said

"The red comes from the blood of the vanquished," Michael said, smiling.

"No, Mars looks red because it has so much iron in the soil."

"The sky is the same color," Rosie said.

"The wind storms on Mars stir the red dust unto the air," Dad said.

Rosie turned to the next page in her atlas. It showed Mars from a distance.

"See those spots and scars in the surface? That is where the Martians tested their proton weapons," Michael said.

"That's not true. Those are ancient volcanoes and canyons," Dad said.

"Mars has the biggest volcano in the solar system. Olympus Mons is three times taller than Mount Everest. It also has canyons that make The Grand Canyon look like a drainage ditch."

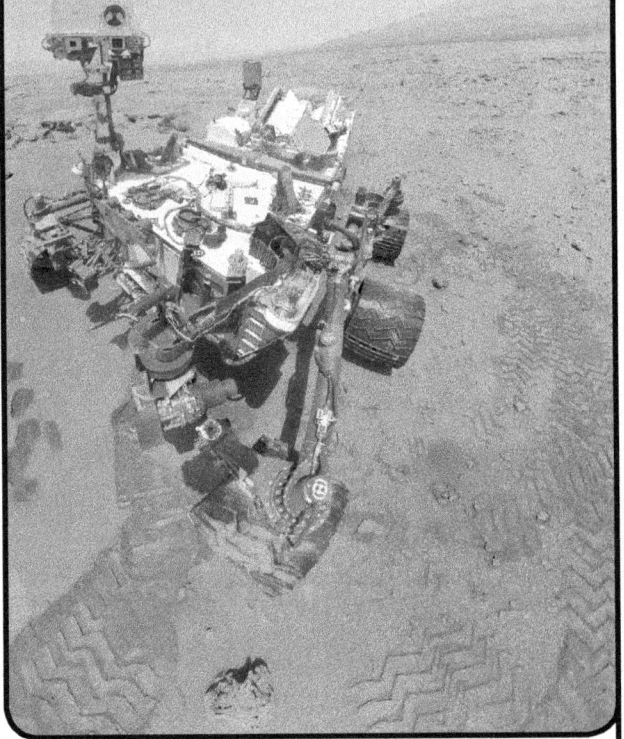

Space probe Curiosity on Mars

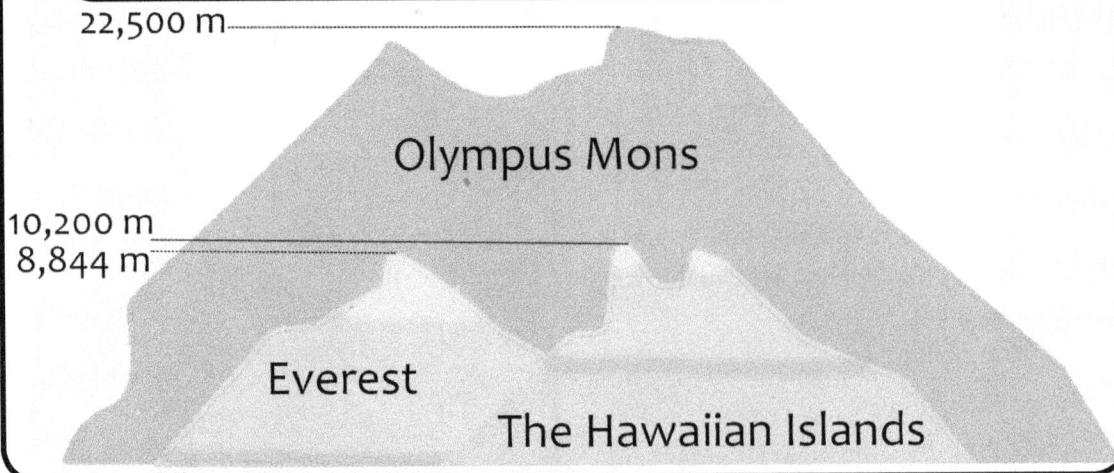

Mars' Olympus Mons compared to Earth's tallest mountains

22,500 m

Olympus Mons

10,200 m
8,844 m

Everest

The Hawaiian Islands

Mars Word Search

```
W M M A R T I A N R
D A X V O L C A N O
U R Z G V X P G W U
S S I C E C A P S R
T Q N O R U Z K Q E
X R P L R A X I S D
Z D V D T W Z J X Q
C U R I O S I T Y W
```

Mars
martian
axis
cold

ice caps
curiosity
red

dust
volcano
rover

Mars

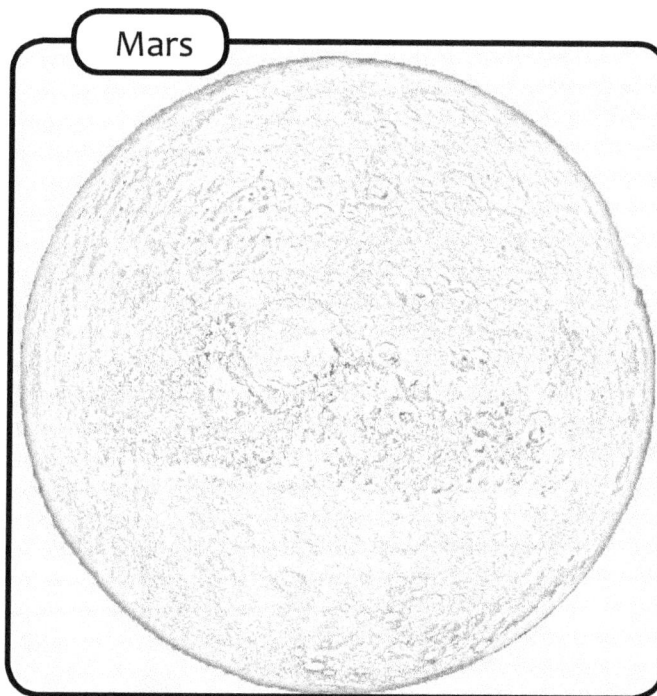

Mars Word Search

banana
flute
french bread
pencil
smiley face

ice cream
pizza
phone
ruler

Jupiter

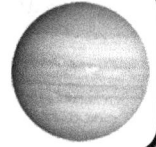

Jane stirred a pot of tomato sauce on the stove.

Rosie measured out a spoonful of spices and added them to the pot. The green specks floated around the bubbling sauce.

Next she added a cube of butter. It floated on the surface for a moment before sinking.

"That's like the giant red spot on Jupiter," Rosie said.

"What are you talking about?" Jane asked.

Rosie pulled out her pocket space atlas and showed Jane a picture of Jupiter.

"See that spot?"

"What is that?" Jane asked.

Michael walked by at that moment. "That is a giant hurricane. It is bigger than the earth. It has been storming for hundreds of years."

"That can't be true. Storms don't last that long."

Dad walked through the kitchen and tasted the sauce. "Jupiter's great red spot has been churning a long time."

"How has it lasted so long?" Rosie asked.

"Scientists are not sure. It may have to do with the high winds in Jupiter's atmosphere."

"Jupiter is a gas giant," Rosie read from her atlas.

She looked up. "Does that mean it is made out of gas?"

"It is made of hydrogen and helium gas. The clouds of gas churn around the planet in giant bands."

"If it is made out of gas, does that mean Jupiter is like a big cloud?" Rosie asked.

Jupiter

"It is more dense than a cloud. Jupiter is so massive, the lower layers of gas are under extreme pressure. That pressure turns the gas to liquid. This pressure also generates heat. Jupiter makes more heat than it receives from the sun."

"Jupiter is the biggest planet in the solar system," Rosie said.

"That's right. It is giant. It is more massive than all the other planets put together," Dad said.

"Since it is so big, it must have long days," Rosie said.

"It only takes ten hours for Jupiter to turn on its axis," Dad said.

"That's fast," Rosie said.

"The fast rotation makes the planet bulge out at its equator."

"Kind of like you," Michael said patting Dad's stomach.

"Thanks," Dad replied.

"If it spins so fast. Does it have any moons?" Rosie asked.

"Astronomers have discovered more than 60 moons around Jupiter," Dad said.

"Jupiter is so big that many comets, asteroids, and Martians get caught in its pull," Michael said.

"There are no Martians," Rosie said.

"Jupiter has captured many moons. Yet at least eight of the moons formed at the same time as Jupiter."

"How do scientists know?" Rosie asked.

"Those moons are bigger than the others. They more round and have more regular orbits."

"I bet you need a super telescope to see moons around a planet so far away," Rosie said.

"Four of Jupiter's moons are near the size of the earth's moon. Galileo, a scientist in the 1600's, first discovered them."

"Ganymede, Jupiter's largest moon is also the largest moon in the solar system. Many icy craters cover the moon Callisto. Io has active volcanoes. Europa is covered with ice that has cracked in a distinctive crisscross pattern."

"I wish we could send space missions to Jupiter's moons," Rosie said.

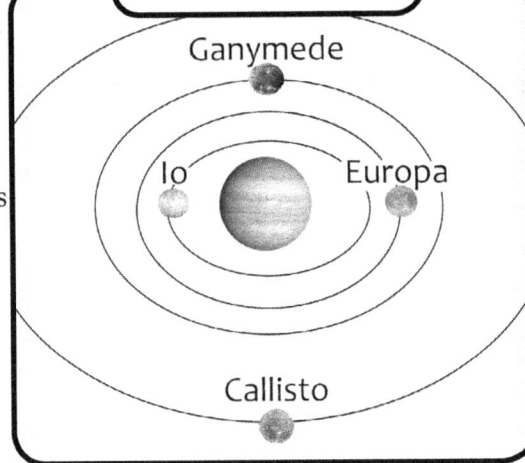

Galilean moons

Ganymede

Io   Europa

Callisto

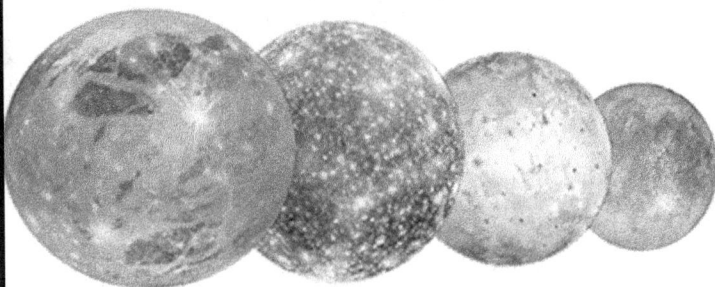

Jupiter's Galilean Moons

Ganymede   Callisto   Europa   Io

Jupiter Word Scramble

PEARUO   _____

GYRDHNEO   _____

TIVGYAR   _____

MEEYGNAD   _____

IMHLEU   _____

TIJERPU   _____

EARGT DER POST   _____

LISTCOLA   _____

Jupiter

Jupiter Hidden Picture

bread, pizza, banana, mug, bowling ball, smiley face, heart, ruler, paint brush, snail

Saturn

The family went to a pool party. They swam, ate, and played games.

Rosie's dad took a handful of hula hoops and called the children over.

"Whoever can hula hoop the longest wins a prize," Dad said.

Michael, Rosie and Jane each took a hula hoop. On the count of three, they spun the hoops around their waists.

Michael and Rosie soon dropped their hoops, but Jane spun and spun.

Rosie watched in awe. After nearly thirty seconds, Rosie said, "She reminds me of Saturn."

"Did you bring your space atlas to the pool?" Michael asked with disbelief.

"Everyone knows that Saturn has rings."

"Yes, Saturn has bright rings. But did you know they used to think Saturn had handles or ears."

"Why?"

"Saturn was so far away, they couldn't see it clearly." Dad said. "It wasn't until Christiaan Huygens invented a better telescope, they could see they were rings."

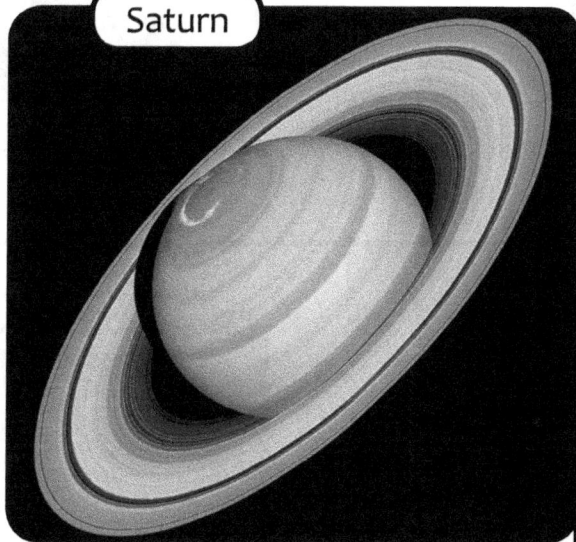

Saturn

Jane dropped her hula hoop when she realized no one was watching.

"What is my prize?" she asked.

Dad picked up the other hoops and put them all around her. "You get to spin all the hoops."

"OK," She said.

Jane did her best, but couldn't spin them for long.

"If I was bigger I could do it," Jane said.

"Saturn keeps all it rings in line because it is so massive," Dad said.

"It is the second biggest planet," Rosie added.

"Saturn is made up of hydrogen and helium, elements that are lighter than air. Inside Saturn is molten hydrogen and an iron core. Saturn is the least dense of the planets. It is even less dense than water."

Dad picked up a beach ball.

"So if you could throw the planet Saturn into a big pool, it would float," he said.

Dad threw the ball into the pool, splashing the kids with water.

"What about the rings? Would they float too?"

"The rings are made of rocks, ice and dust. Some of the rocks are as big as a house and some are as small as a grain of rice."

"Does Saturn have moons?"

"Saturn has many moons. One of it's moons, Titan, is the second largest moon in the solar system."

Saturn's Rings

"Scientists recently sent a probe to Titan," Dan added.

"Titan is the only rocky moon with a thick atmosphere. That makes is similar to earth. They wanted to see below the clouds."

"To see if there is life on Titan? Did they find any?"

"They found liquid methane lakes and a nitrogen atmosphere. Scientists think it is similar to earth's early years except it is much colder."

Titan's thick atmosphere

Saturn Word Search

```
N  X  R  E  J  R  L  F  P  D
H  R  C  Q  X  R  I  N  G  S
U  D  H  Y  D  R  O  G  E  N
Y  E  Z  T  I  T  A  N  P  P
G  N  S  U  R  F  A  C  E  L
E  S  A  T  U  R  N  W  S  A
N  I  T  R  O  G  E  N  K  N
S  T  E  L  E  S  C  O  P  E
B  Y  I  N  I  S  S  A  C  T
```

Saturn   rings   hydrogen
density   titan   surface
telescope   Cassini   planet
Huygens   nitrogen

Saturn

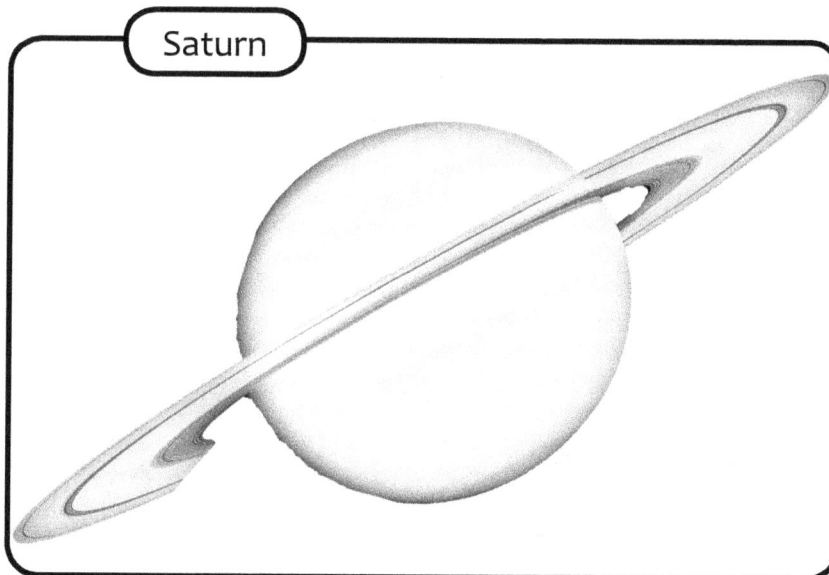

Saturn Maze

Fill in the blanks with the following words:
thick, ice, seventh, hydrogen, rocks, dust, Titan

Saturn is the _____ planet from the sun.

It has bright rings made of _____, _____ and_____

Its biggest moon is named _____

This moon has a _____ atmosphere

Saturn is made up mostly of_____ gas.

Uranus

Rosie and her dad were at the county fair. She nibbled a snow cone to keep cool in the summer heat.

They walked by the animal exhibits. Rosie noticed one of the cows was named Uranus.

"Uranus is the 7th planet from the sun," Rosie said.

"That's right," Dad said.

"What is it like?" Rosie asked.

"It is so far away, scientists don't know much about it," Dad said.

"Is it icy?" she asked.

"It is colder than you can imagine. It is so cold that gas in the atmosphere is frozen solid."

"I thought it was a gas giant like Jupiter and Saturn," Rosie said.

"Scientists like to call Uranus an ice giant instead of a gas giant. It is made of gas, but 80% of the gas is ice," Dad said. "Uranus is twice as far away as Saturn. It takes 84 years for Uranus to circle the sun."

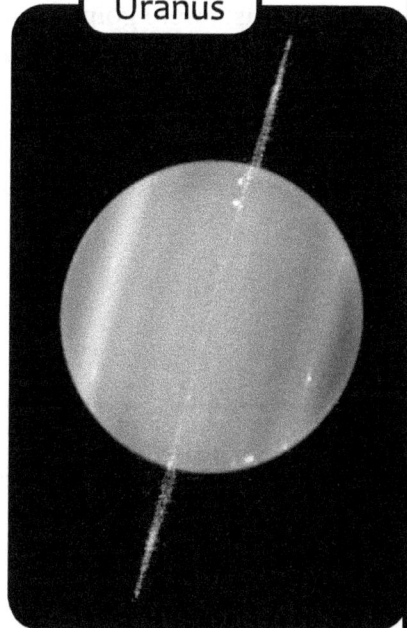

Uranus

"That is a long time," Rosie said. She took another bite of her snow cone. "What else do scientists know about it?"

"They know it has crazy days," Dad said.

"What do you mean?"

"It's axis is tipped 90 degrees. So that means the poles have 42-year-long days."

"It is tipped so far over, it is like a ball rolling around the sun," Dad added.

"Why is it so different from the other planets?" Rosie asked.

"Scientists think a large object hit Uranus after it was formed. The impact set Uranus spinning in the wrong direction."

They walked by more fair booths. One booth had little rubber ducks floating in a steel bathtub. Rosie paid $5 for a chance to shoot the ducks with a water gun. If she tipped a duck over she would win a prize.

Rosie tried her best, but she could only make the ducks spin.

"It's OK," Rosie's dad consoled. "They give you little water guns on purpose. It would take a water cannon to make those ducks tip. Just like Uranus, it takes a lot of force to get something to leave it's natural state."

The two walked past the midway and sat in the shade.

"Can you see Uranus in the sky?"

"You can see it if you know what you are looking for. It is so dim and slow moving, astronomers thought it was a star for a long time. In 1783, Sir William Herschel described Uranus as a comet. But after more study, scientists decided it was a planet," Dad said.

"Did he come up with it's name?" Rosie asked.

"Herschel wanted to name the planet after King George."

"I like the name George," Rosie said.

"Only the British liked the name George so scientists settled on the name Uranus. In mythology, Uranus is Saturn's father and Jupiter's grandfather."

"That fits better I guess," Rosie said.

"Uranus has rings. They are darker and thinner than Saturn's rings. They are so hard to see, they were discovered by accident," Dad said.

"By accident?"

"Scientists were going to study Uranus' atmosphere as it passed in front of a distant star. The star's light dimmed a few times before it passed behind Uranus. That is how they found out there were rings."

"Does Uranus have lots of moons like Saturn and Jupiter?" Rosie asked.

"Yes. It has at least 27 moons. Its biggest moons are Titania, Oberon, Miranda, Ariel and Umbriel."

"At least the moons have pretty names," Rosie said.

Some of Uranus' Moons

Oberon

Titiana

Miranda

The Outer Planets • Uranus

Uranus Code

Use the code to decipher the code.

Key

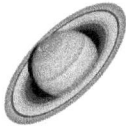

ice	on	a	giant

Uranus	is	that	planet

side	tipped	its	blue

Uranus True/False

_____Uranus is bigger than Saturn.

_____Uranus is tipped 90 degrees.

_____William Herschel discovered Uranus.

_____Herschel want to name Uranus after King George

_____Uranus is 20% ice.

_____Uranus takes 24 years to orbit the sun.

_____Uranus has rings.

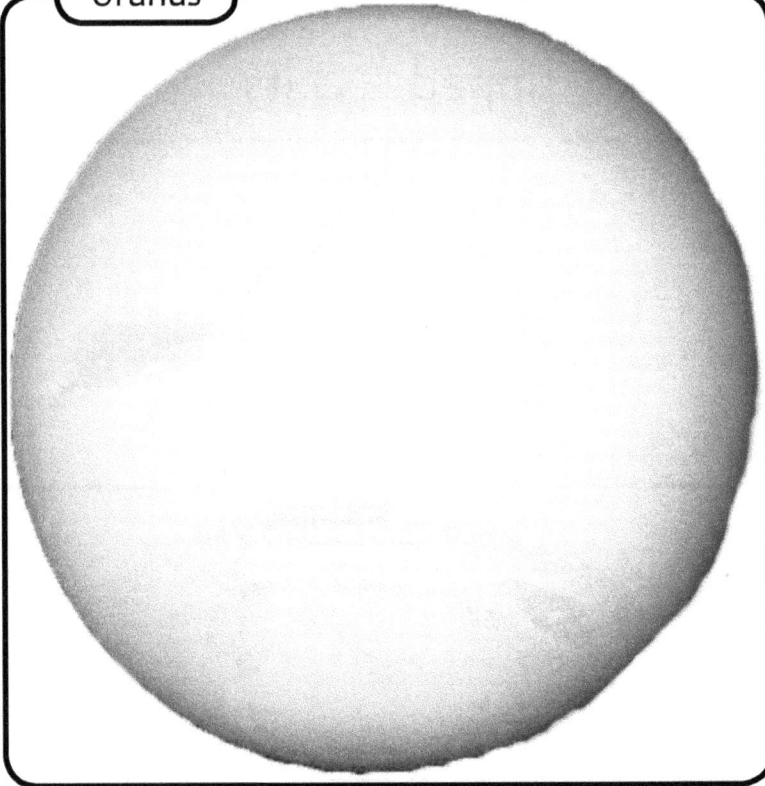

Uranus

Neptune

The kids were playing in the backyard after dinner.

"Let's play planet tag," Rosie suggested.

Jane and Michael sighed.

"We play that all the time," Jane cried.

Michael started for the house.

"Play tag with your sister," Dad said. "Or you can start weeding."

"Fine," Michael said. "But I get to be the sun this time. Spinning like a planet makes me dizzy."

Rosie and Jane spun around Michael. He tried to catch them without moving.

At one point, Rosie and Jane got too close. They almost hit each other.

"That would never happen to real planets," Michael said. "They are too far apart to pull on each other."

"Sometimes they do affect each other. That was how astronomers discovered Neptune," Dad said. "Scientists noticed Uranus' orbit was irregular. They thought the pull of an unknown planet's gravity might be causing it. Astronomers were able to guess where the unknown planet was based on Uranus' orbit. Sure enough, they soon found the culprit was Neptune."

"Why didn't they just see Neptune moving in the sky?" Rosie asked.

"It is too far from the sun. Telescopes weren't very good back in the 1800's. It would take a lot of luck to find a planet that far away without any clues." Dad said.

Dizzy from spinning, Rosie fell to the ground. She took out her space atlas.

"Neptune is a blue ice giant. It takes 165 years to orbit the sun."

"That is a long time. It has only orbited the sun once since it has been discovered," Dad said.

"It has white methane clouds," Rosie read.

Neptune

"It also has high winds and storms like Jupiter. It has one storm bigger than the rest. They

call it the 'Great Dark Spot' because it was like Jupiter's 'Great Red Spot'," Dad said.

"If Neptune is frozen, how does it have storms?" Rosie asked.

"Like Saturn and Jupiter, its inner core is hot. It also has a strong yet erratic magnetic field."

Rosie read from her atlas. "Triton is Neptune's biggest moon."

"Triton is the only moon in the solar system that turns the wrong way," Dad said.

"What do you mean?" she asked.

Triton

"Most moons rotate the same direction its planet spins. Triton doesn't. Scientists think it may be a captured dwarf planet."

"What is a dwarf planet?" Rosie asked.

"Dwarf planets are smaller than the moon," Michael said.

"They orbit the sun. They have enough mass that they are spheres," Dad said.

"Pluto is a dwarf planet," Michael said.

"Is it the only dwarf planet?" Rosie asked.

"No. There are five official dwarf planets. They are named Pluto, Ceres, Eris, Haumea, and Makemake. There are other asteroids that could be dwarf planets. As we learn more about them, they may get added to the list. With our improved telescopes and good luck, we could find many others out there too."

Moon Matching
Match the moon with its planet.

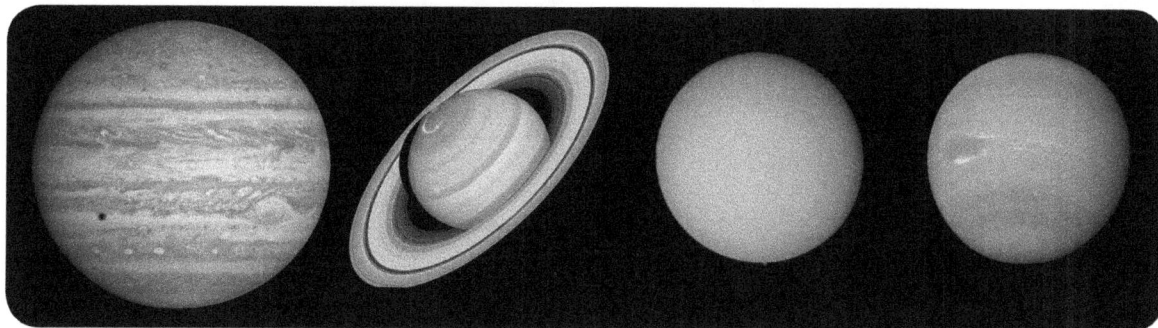

Jupiter   Saturn   Uranus   Neptune

Triton	Oberon
Io	Ariel
Titan	Titania
Ganymede	Umbriel
Callisto	Europa

Neptune Word Scramble

TEEPNUN   _____

WADFR   _____

NORITT   _____

POLSEPOTE _____

VITYRAG   _____

LATEPN   _____

RIOBT   _____

TANEEHM   _____

Neptune

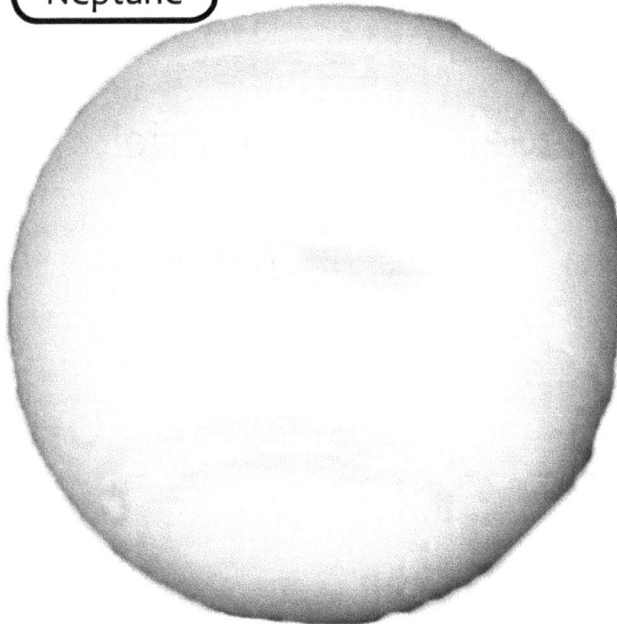

Asteroids

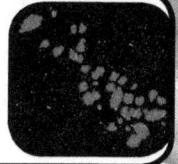

Rosie watched Michael play a video game.

"What are you playing?" Rosie asked.

"Shhh," Michael said.

Dad walked by. "You're playing Asteroid. I loved this game when I was a kid."

"I read about asteroids in my pocket space atlas but these don't look like the ones in my book." Rosie said.

"They don't have to look real. It's a fun game," Michael said.

"There are more than 750,000 asteroids in the Solar system," Rosie read from her atlas.

"I only have 749,000 left to go," Michael said.

"The average distance between asteroids is about 600,000 miles," Dad said.

"Would you guys be quiet?"

Dad whispered to Rosie. "The rocks in that game are much too big. Most asteroids are small. They wouldn't crush a space ship. They would only ding the windshield,"

"These asteroids are all that is left of the planet the aliens destroyed," Michael said.

"It wasn't a real planet then," Rosie said.

"Some scientist think there could have been a planet between Mars and Jupiter. "

"What happened to it?" Rosie asked.

"The gravity from Jupiter broke it up. The asteroids belt is all that is left of it." Dad said.

"You know this is just a game right? You don't have to figure out where the asteroids came from. You just shoot them." Dan said.

"Ceres, Vesta, Pallas and Hygiea are big asteroids," Rosie read from her atlas.

"The four biggest asteroids weigh more than the rest of them combined." Rosie's dad said.

"They could be Trojan Asteroids," Dad said.

"What are Trojan Asteroids?" Rosie asked.

"They are asteroids that share Jupiter's orbit. There are two main clouds of them, 60 degrees before and 60 degrees behind Jupiter."

"Are they more dangerous? Would you need to shoot them?" Rosie asked.

"They are about the same density as the main asteroid belt," Dad said. "You could easily

dodge them with a space ship."

"You two need to leave," Michael said.

"They could be Trans-Neptunian objects," Dad said.

"Where are those?" Rosie asked.

"They are the asteroids beyond Neptune's orbit. Scientist don't know how many TNO's there are."

Michael rolled his eyes. "I think it is a safe to say there is a lot of empty space out beyond Neptune."

Dad snapped his fingers. "I know, it's the Oort cloud."

"What is the Oort Cloud?" Rosie asked.

"It is the area at the edge of the solar system. It is where the comets originate. Scientist think there could be trillions of objects out there."

"That could be it," Rosie said.

"The Oort cloud is too far away. You would never get a ship out there."

Michael paused his game and glared at them. "This game is completely fictional. It is based on the idea of asteroids. It couldn't happen anywhere in our solar system."

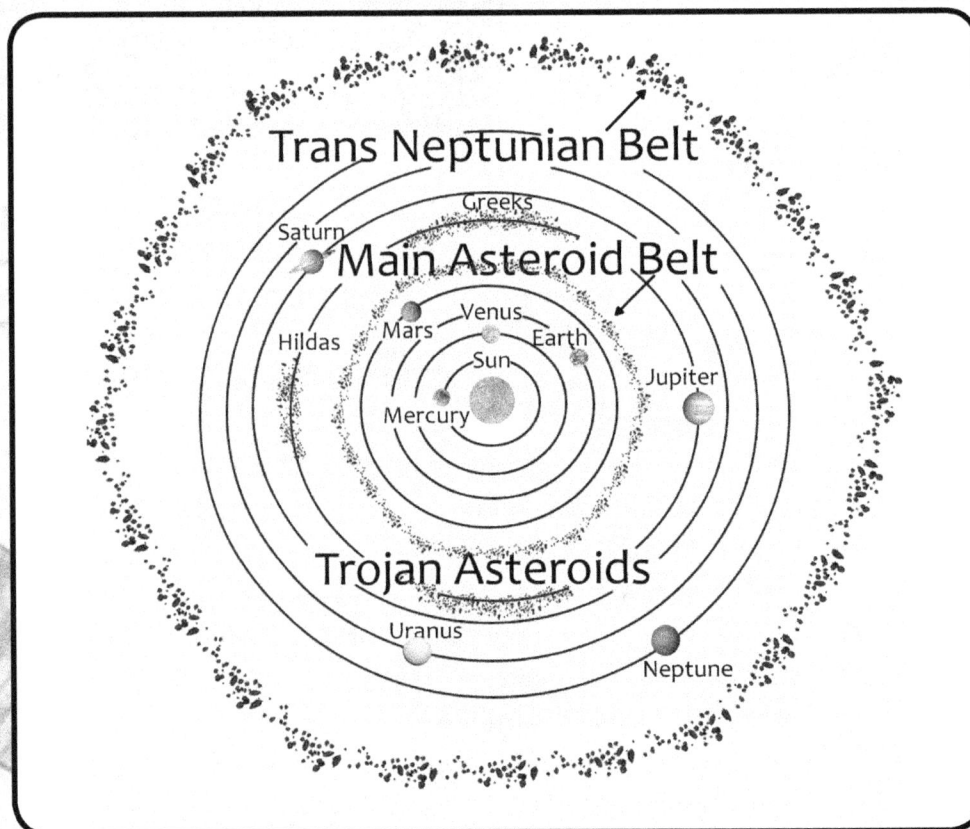

Asteroid Matching

Fill in the blank with T for "Trojan", M for "main asteroid belt," O for "Oort cloud" or N for "neither"

___These asteroids are between Mars and Jupiter.

___These asteroids are beyond the orbit of Neptune.

___There are billions of these asteroids.

___The asteroid Ceres in among these.

___These asteroids are in Jupiter's orbit.

___This group of asteroids is so crowded they are always hitting each other.

___These asteroids could be the remains of a planet.

Asteroid Vesta

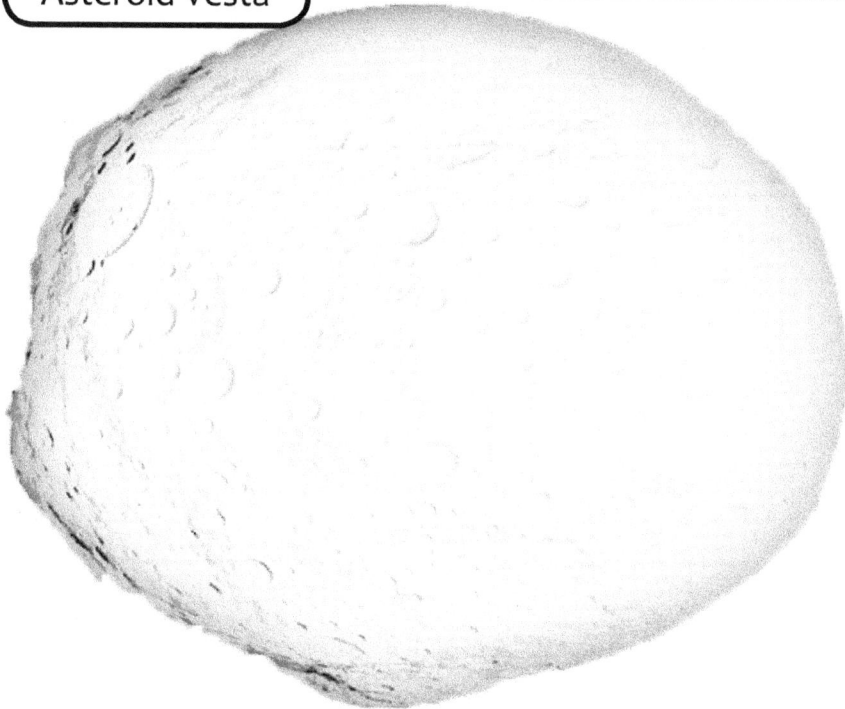

Asteroid Code
Use the key to decode the message.

Key

is between	Main	Jupiter and Mars

belt	orbits of	asteroid	the

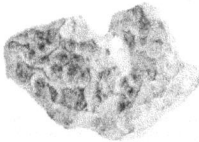   

_____

 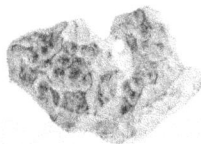  

_____

Meteors

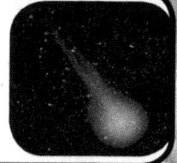

The family went to the Independence Day celebration at the park.

"I love fireworks," Dad said. "They are like falling stars."

Rosie turned to him, alarmed. "Stars don't really fall do they?"

"No. It is just an expression. Real falling stars are called meteors. Meteors are small space rocks that fall into earth's atmosphere."

"Are they dangerous?" she asked.

"Not usually. They are so small that they burn up long before they hit the ground."

"Can we see them?"

"We can't see the space rocks, but we can see their fiery trails as they shoot across the sky," Dad said.

"I would love to see one. Where can I look?"

"Meteors fall all the time. But they are hard to predict. The best chance to see one is to find out when the annual meteor showers are."

"When are they?"

Perseid Meteor

"Meteor showers happen about once a month. The brightest showers are the Perseids in August, the Leonids in November and the Orionids in October," Rosie's dad said.

"Do you need a telescope to see them?" Rosie asked.

"No. All you need is a clear night, low moonlight, and lots of patience."

"Kind of like waiting for the fireworks to start?"

"It is similar. Although meteor showers are much slower than fireworks. The most active meteor showers have only 100 meteors per hour. Most have less than 10 per hour."

"Do they shine over the whole sky?" Rosie asked.

"They can be all over the sky, but they all appear to come from the same point in the sky."

"Meteor showers are named after the constellation they radiate from. Then just add the ending 'id'. People in ancient times thought the showers were like children of the constellations. For example, the Orionids radiate from the constellation Orion," Dad said.

"So 'id' means kid," Rosie said.

"That's right."

"Where do the meteors showers come from?" Rosie asked.

"Every year the earth passes through debris fields as it orbits the sun. The debris are from comets that have passed through earth's orbit."

"Do meteors ever reach the ground?" Rosie asked.

"Yes. When a meteor hits the ground it is called a meteorite. Small meteorites hit the earth all the time." Dad said.

"How would I know if I found one?" Rosie asked and she looked through the grass.

"Most meteorites will stick to a strong magnet. They also are very heavy for their size."

"Rosie held up some small pebbles. "Do you think any of theses are meteorites?"

"You would be very lucky if you found one. Most meteors burn up in the atmosphere before they reach the ground." Dad said.

"Big meteorites would be easier to find." Rosie said.

"Maybe. The big meteorites make impact craters like you see on the moon."

Impact Crater

Stony Meteorite found in Antarctica

"Does the earth have any craters?" Rosie asked.

"There are some. Most have eroded over time. Some scientists think a giant meteorite may have caused the extinction of the dinosaurs."

Rosie's eyes widened.

"But that is rare. You wouldn't have to worry about that happening any time soon."

Meteor Word Search
Find the hidden words in the puzzle.

```
S   Q   W   T   C   A   P   I   W
Y   Z   R   O   E   T   E   M   D
N   C   R   A   T   E   R   S   K
O   R   J   K   M   Y   S   V   Q
T   X   S   H   O   W   E   R   M
S   S   L   E   O   N   I   D   S
O   R   I   O   N   I   D   S   H
V   A   U   P   L   J   S   F   L
```

craters   stony
impact   meteor
Orionids   shower
Perseids   moon
Leonids

Meteor Maze

Find your way to the center of the impact crater.

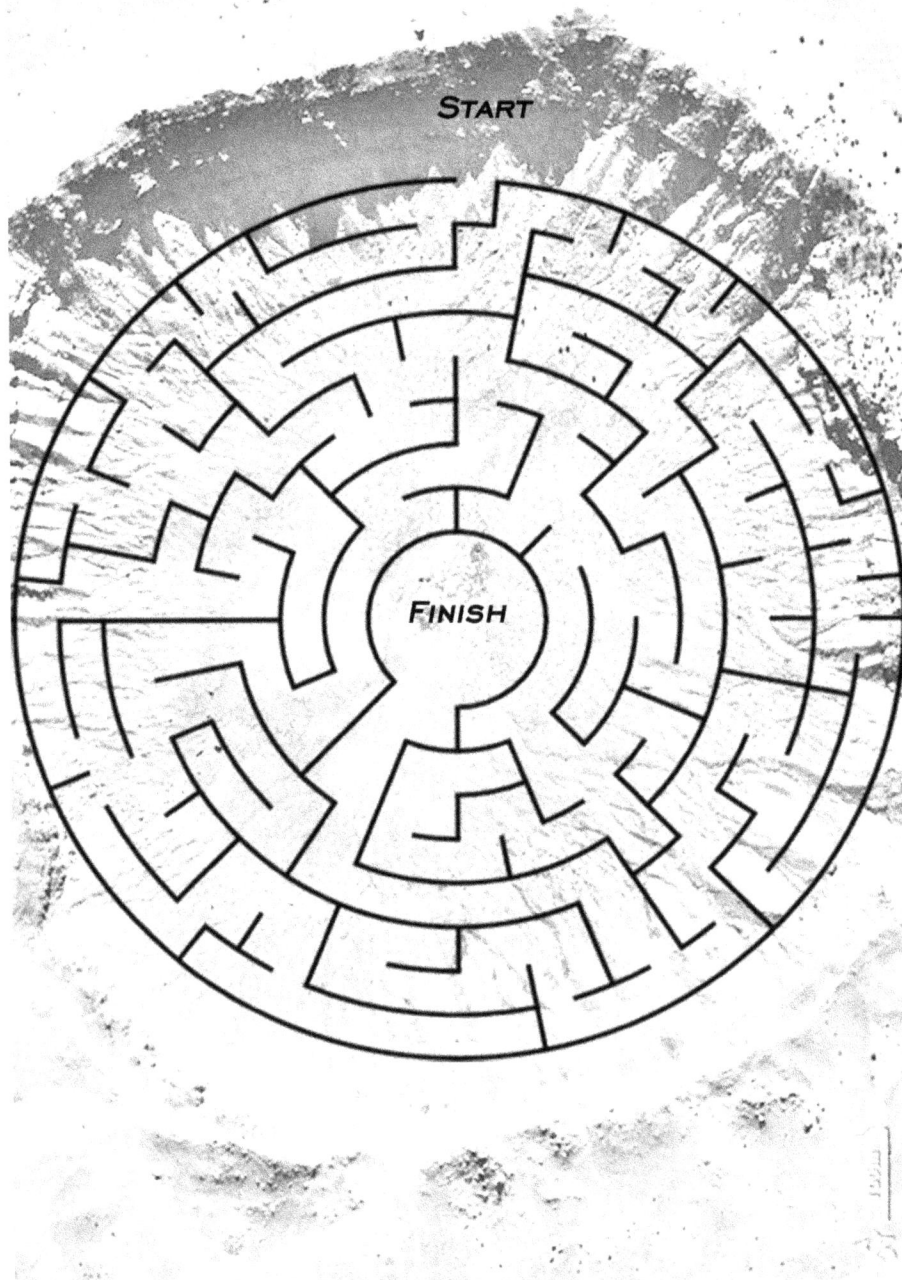

START

FINISH

Comets

One evening, Dad took the kids outside to play. He showed them a new game called 'comet tail'.

"It's just a tennis ball in a sock," Jane said.

"It's still cool," he said. "Now spread out."

The kids stepped back.

"See if you can catch it with the tail," Dad said after he threw it up in the air.

Michael caught the first throw.

"Good," Dad said. "Now throw it back."

Soon all the kids were able to catch and throw the 'comet tail'.

After dusk fell, the older kids went inside to do homework but Rosie stayed outside.

Comet

"You're thinking about real comets aren't you?" Dad asked.

"When I throw it by the tail, the ball always lands first," Rosie said. Then she showed him by throwing the comet tail. It zoomed high over head and then came back to the ground, ball first.

"I see," he said. "Real comets are like that too. Their tails always points away from the sun."

"Why?" Rosie asked.

"The sun has energy that radiates outward all the time. It's called the solar wind. That wind blows the comet tails outward."

"What are the tails made from?" Rosie asked.

"They are made gas or dust that is melting off the comet," Dad said.

"Comets melt?"

"They are coming from the outer reaches of the solar system where it is extremely cold. As they get closer to the sun, they start to melt."

"Are they like snowballs?"

"More like dirty snowballs. As they melt, the dust and gases inside them blow off into

space."

"If you look closely, you can often see two tails on a comet. One is the gas tail and one is the dust tail," Dad said.

"How do they know what the tails are made of?" Rosie asked.

"NASA has sent probes to a few comets. One probe called 'Stardust' even returned a sample back to earth."

"Scientist know where to find comets?" Rosie asked as she tossed the comet tail up in the sky again.

"Some comets are predictable. They come around every hundred years or so."

"That's not very often."

"They may not be often, but they are memorable. Halley's comet returns to earth every 76 years. People wrote about the comet in their histories. Now we use the records of the sightings of Halley's comet to date important historical events. "

Comet tails point away from the sun

Comet Orbit

Earth's Orbit

Sun

"I will probably never see a comet," Rosie said.

"You never know when an one will show up. Astronomers don't know all the comets that are out there," Dad said.

"Have you ever seen a comet?"

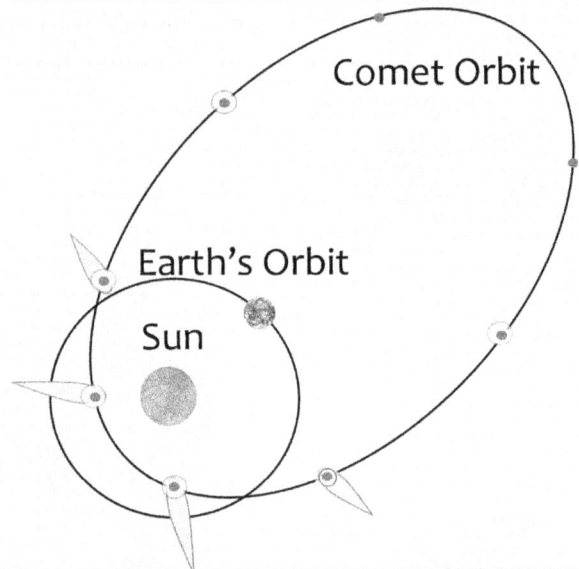

Bayeux Tapestry with Halley's Comet

MIRAN T STELLA

HAROLD

"I saw a couple comets back in the 1990's. One called Hyakutake, and one called Hale-Bopp. They were the brightest thing in the sky for months."

"Those are funny names," Rosie said.

"They were named after the people who discovered them."

"Maybe I will discover a comet someday," Rosie said.

"I'm sure you will," Dad said.

Comet word scramble

Unscramble the letters to form words from the story.

LYALHE _____

ILTA _____

MEOTC _____

STSDATRU _____

YAKKATHUE _____

LABWONSSL _____

TEEIDPRBCLA _____

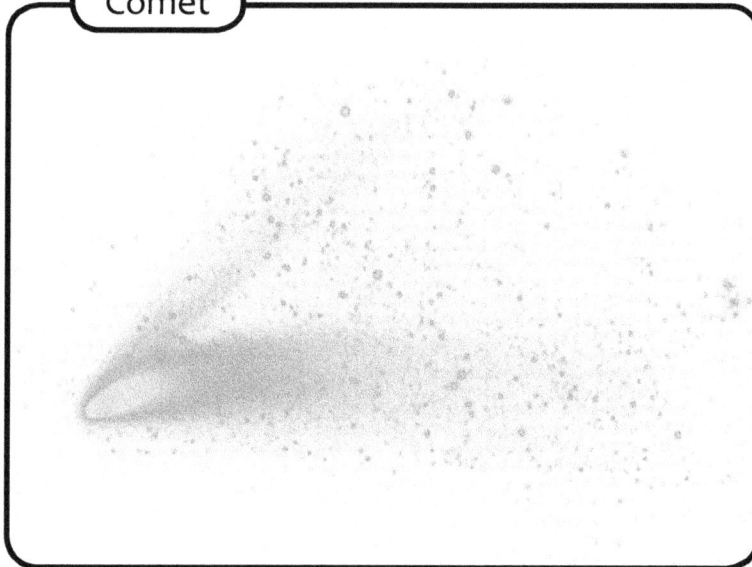

Comet

Comet Hidden Picture

Find the following objects hidden in the picture:

Pizza, ruler, bowling ball, smiley face, pencil, funnel, book, bread, fish, cherry

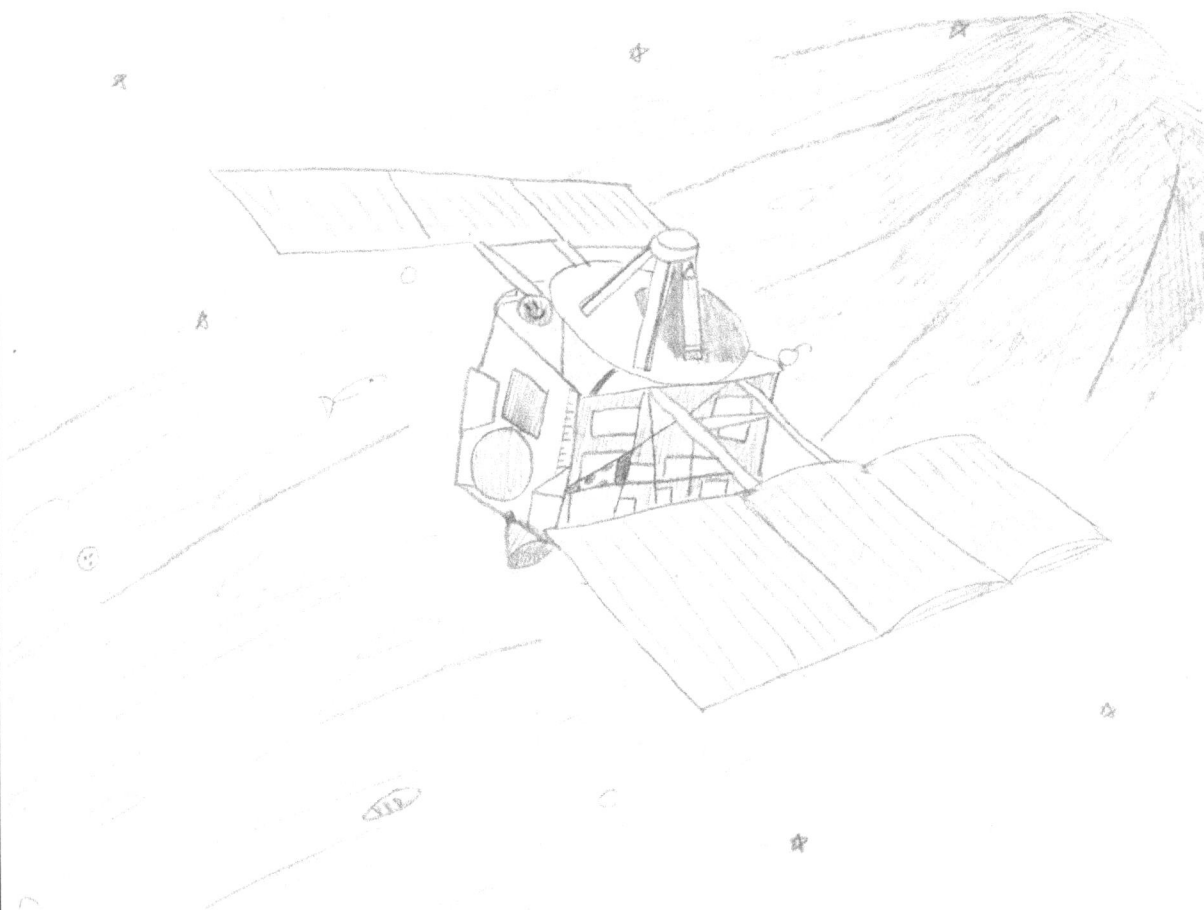

The Stardust probe brought back
samples from the _____ comet.

About the author:

Diane Kirkpatrick graduated from BYU in 1996 with a BS in Microbiology. She has homeschooled her children for many years. After struggling to find an easy and affordable science program, she was inspired to write this book.

From the Author:

I hope you enjoyed this book.

If you have any question or concerns please email: waterglenpress@waterglen.net

For more info on future titles in this series visit: waterglenpress.wordpress.com

To download activity sheets go to http://waterglenpress.wordpress.com/downloads/

Image Credits

Images: pages 1,5,9, 14, 18, 41, 49, 53, 62, 63, 69, 70, 73: 123RF Stock Photo

Diagrams and drawings: pages 2, 6, 8, 10,12, 13, 15, 17, 20, 21,22, 24, 25, 26, 28, 29, 30, 31, 32, 33, 34,38, 42, 46, 48, 50, 52, 58, 65, 66, 74, 75, 76: Melissa Kirkpatrick

Images: pages 37, 42, 44, 45, 46, 54, 57, 61, 70, 74: NASA

www.ingramcontent.com/pod-product-compliance
Lightning Source LLC
Chambersburg PA
CBHW080526030426
42337CB00023B/4646